The Coldest Night

The Coldest Night

A Family's Experience of Suicide

Carol Anne Milton

VERITAS

This edition published 2009 by
Veritas Publications
7–8 Lower Abbey Street
Dublin 1, Ireland
Email publications@veritas.ie
Website www.veritas.ie

ISBN 978 1 84730 202 1
Copyright © Carol Anne Milton, 2009

10 9 8 7 6 5 4 3 2 1

A catalogue record for this book is available from the
British Library.
Lines from 'Lovely Young One' by Christy Moore used
with permission.
Cover photograph taken by Stephen Milton.

Printed in the Republic of Ireland by ColourBooks Ltd, Dublin

Veritas books are printed on paper made from the wood pulp
of managed forests. For every tree felled, at least one tree is
planted, thereby renewing natural resources.

Dedicated to my children,
David, Stephen, Niall, Alan and Noelle,
who will always be the source of my most profound joy.

Acknowledgements

I would like to thank the following people who were instrumental in helping me write this book:

Dr Bernadette Flanagan, Head of Research at All Hallows College, formerly of Milltown Institute, who introduced me to Maura Hyland, Director of Veritas Publications, because she thought I had something important to share with others.

Donna Doherty of Veritas, who believed in me and encouraged me all the way through, and who refused to allow me to give up on this project.

Noel and our family, for contributing their thoughts and feelings about losing Alan and moving on, whether written or not. Also to Frances, who so readily agreed to share her memory of the time of Alan's death, and to Íde for being willing to revisit the painful memory of losing a boyfriend whom she loved so much. I know how difficult it was for all of you to go back to that time and I am deeply grateful.

Contents

Introduction

Sometimes we hear people refer jokingly to a 'past life', for example, 'In a past life I was a such-and-such', meaning one had a previous career or relationship. For me there really are two distinct lives: my life prior to the death of my son, Alan, and the radically changed life my family and I had to learn to live following his death by suicide in 2002. When I look back on my life before that event – what I see as my own 'past life' – it was a relatively comfortable and secure life with the normal ups and downs, joyful and sad occasions, births, marriages and deaths that are part of everyone's life – the times of calm and the times of turmoil that exist in every family. My world consisted of my immediate family, my retreat work with young people, my extended family and my friends.

I felt blessed with my four sons, David, Stephen, Niall and Alan, and my daughter, Noelle, who at fifteen was showing signs of growing into a lovely young woman. My sons had all grown into intelligent, generous and compassionate men, aware of the needs of the world around them, but at the same time full of the mischief, exuberance and frequent outrageousness of young adulthood. My children had been my greatest source of joy since they were born and my gratitude to God for them flowed into a desire to work with young people, which I have been doing now for eighteen years.

Surrounding these elements of my life was, and is, my deep faith in a great and powerful Other, whom I call God – a word that I have long ago ceased to grapple with the meaning of and so am content to call the 'Unnamable'; something that is within me and within all living things. Many years ago I read somewhere the lines: 'God and I are a majority; no force can overcome us.' This stayed with me; I knew what it meant with my mind, however, today I know it with my heart and spirit. For me it is a truth because I am healthy and alive today. There is a permanent scar from the pain of the loss of my youngest son, but also a renewed capacity to feel joyful and to live life to the full having survived the horrendous evil that is the suicide of a beloved child.

I have written this book for parents, educators, pastors and for every young person who thinks that his/her life is not worth living and that he/she is not worth loving. It is written in order to tell the story of survival after the suicide of one's child, as well as to pass on information from my research into suicide and depression and how nurturing a healthy spirituality could go some way towards combating suicide being looked at as an option.

In the book I have moved from a personal account of the details of Alan's death to sharing my journey of research, questioning and my attempt at understanding depression among young males and why it is that a growing number of these complete suicide.

In the first three chapters I have described what it was like to hear that Alan had taken his life. Included here are the personal memories of that time contributed by my daughter, Noelle, my sons, David and Niall, Alan's girlfriend, Íde, and his godmother, Frances, who is also my cousin and friend.

Chapter four describes what it was like for us in the first weeks and months following Alan's death and how we had to learn to construct a changed life after losing a family member. Chapter five explores the features, forms and some common myths surrounding depressive illness, and chapter six examines suicide in a similar way. Chapter seven looks at the 'why' of suicide in an attempt to answer the unanswerable question.

In chapter eight I attempt to explore suicide from a spiritual perspective and to explain my belief that a healthy spirituality leads to a healthy self-esteem, an increased sense of our value and purpose in the world and how this helps me to live a life that is joyful and fulfilled. Finally, chapter nine deals with moving on from grief and the personal reflections of my family regarding how they have coped with a changed life after Alan's death.

One voice must lead the chorus that is represented in this book, but I feel that it is important to include the reflections of family members in order that the reader may receive a more complete account of our journey through bereavement and the grieving process. I hope that this doesn't interrupt the flow of the book, however, perhaps a parent or teacher reading this will think it worthwhile to show the reflections and reactions of Alan's siblings to young persons in their care. These young people may be able to identify with the feelings expressed here, or may see for themselves the destructive impact that suicide can have on the family and close friends of the deceased.

My deepest hope for young people is that they will come to know the immense value that their lives bring to this world, not their academic or sporting achievements – useful as these are – but how the very fact that they exist can enrich their family, community and the wider world. I hope that they will come to realise their immense power to be co-creators of a world of freedom, justice, truth, beauty and love.

I hope that we, the nurturers of our young people, who are the soul of the next generation, will have the wisdom to prioritise the importance of a healthy self-regard in our children over material success; that we will look within ourselves to discover that Other which provides a deep and authentic self-love, allowing us to love selflessly these precious beings who have been put into our care.

The title of the book was inspired by a poem that Niall wrote immediately following Alan's suicide, and with which I begin this story.

'The Coldest Night'

by Niall Milton

Here I am
Tethered
My blood has stopped its frantic rush
My hands lie still at my sides
The wind caresses my unfeeling skin.

My depth I could not bear
Others' love I could not believe
So I chose this escape
And in my release, I hope
Not for happiness, but for peace.

Perhaps I will be found soon
My solitude ended
I almost see myself
From outside
My body like a ghost in the darkness.

Upon my action
My mind freed from guilt
For family, friend and foe
Freed from regret and pain
Freed from life and learning.

Perhaps I would retract
For the sake of five minutes
Perhaps I ought ...
Perhaps the loss I cause will be fleeting
Then again, perhaps not.

Chapter 1

A Day Like Any Other

'Love knows not its own depth until the hour of separation.'

Kahlil Gibran

Beginning the Day

Friday, 1 March 2002 began as any ordinary day would in our house. By 9 a.m. my husband, Noel, and our sons, Stephen (25) and Niall (24), had left for work. Our daughter, Noelle (15), had gone to school where she would complete her Junior Certificate mock exams that day. Our youngest son, Alan (22), was, I presumed, still asleep. My eldest son, David (28), lived and worked in Copenhagen at the time and has since married and settled in Denmark.

I finished breakfast and sat down in my favourite armchair by the patio doors leading out to the back garden, savouring the silence that ensued when my family had left, after the noise and the rushing around that was normal in our home as everybody prepared for their day. As much as I loved the vitality, the music, the voices, all the sounds and noises of our lively household, I deeply appreciated these times of tranquility, when I could gather my thoughts and prepare for my own day. I remember closing my eyes for a moment and asking for the protection of all my family, something I had done every day since each of them in turn had moved from under my wing and into the wider world of school when they were children.

I was the coordinator of a school retreat team at the time and one of my tasks was to liaise with the religious education departments in schools, so I was waiting for two schools to open in order to finalise arrangements for upcoming retreats. Having made my calls, I was just about to stand up and go into the kitchen when I glanced outside and saw a row of gardaí in yellow jackets moving down the back garden, side by side. There was a garda at the patio door beckoning me around to the front of the house. I opened the front door to find two young gardaí waiting. I invited them in and asked what was going on. One of them replied: 'There's a young lad in a tree in your garden.' My first thought was that a young guy who was trying to escape would not have a chance against the burly gardaí in the garden! Not once in those few seconds did my thoughts turn to anything more sinister.

We went into the room where I had been sitting moments ago and one of the men drew the curtains. The other garda sat beside me on a settee and asked if I had sons. I told him the whereabouts of David, Stephen and Niall, and as I was saying that Alan was upstairs in bed, an odd stirring began in the pit of my stomach. I thought it strange that they didn't stand back, but went ahead of me up the stairs, while I gave directions to Alan's bedroom from behind. I then began to realise that this was no hunt for a runaway youngster, and that 'young lad in the tree' meant something else – something that I would not artic-ulate to myself. By the time I reached the room the cur-tains were drawn here also, as Alan's bedroom faced the back garden of the house. Alan's bed was empty and had not been slept in.

My immediate thought was that he had stayed in his friend's house, but as that was practically next door to our own it didn't make sense. Then I thought he might have stayed in his girlfriend's house, but ruled that out also because she had called late the previous night looking for him. He had gone for a drink with his friends, but would have let me know if he had been going somewhere after that. Standing in Alan's room, my mind searching desperately for possibilities that would explain his empty bed, I could feel my heart beginning to race and my throat constricting. I took a deep breath and told myself to get a grip on this silliness! There had to be a perfectly logical reason why Alan was not in his room. Maybe he had gone for a spin on his bike; maybe he had just gone for a walk. My mind would not accept what I knew in my heart.

Identity Confirmed

Downstairs once more, one of the gardaí asked me to describe Alan, which I did, and the garda said he would go and check outside. I was glad of this, because it would prove once and for all that I was being silly in thinking it could be Alan. Any moment now, Alan would walk in the door having been for a swim. I brightened up: 'That's it! He went for a swim ... or something ... or anything. God, no ... this will be perfectly okay, right?' Confusion. The young garda returned, took my hand and very gently said that from my description, it could be Alan. I told myself that there was still nothing certain so it would be okay. A second later, another garda came into the kitchen holding a bank card. He held it out to me, and as I read Alan's name etched clearly on the card, all hope died. Alan had carried out the final act that he believed would relieve him of the anguish with which he had struggled valiantly for the last three years of his life.

Denial

At that moment, my life and the lives of Noel and our family were irrevocably changed. The *joie de vivre* that I was beginning to recapture after the death of my father and my brother, in 1998 and 1999 respectively, was shattered as the bank card confirming Alan's identity was shown to me. I recall that as soon as I knew that it was Alan, that he really had gone from me, my immediate feeling was one of gratitude to God that Alan had been released at last from the agony of the unpredictable mood swings, the crippling anxiety and the periods of depression, which had dogged his life for years. This was a very fleeting sense of gratitude, barely lasting a second, and I have wondered why I can remember it so clearly, or indeed how I could feel grateful at all in a situation so terrible. I have learned since that this is quite a common initial reaction; that when depression, despair and previous suicide attempts have been experienced by a family, there may be relief following the final successful attempt, because the deceased is no longer in despair and the constant threat of suicide is over.

I only have snippets of memory of the time following this and I am inclined to confuse the sequence of events, but I do remember trying – and failing – to swing into 'mother mode', wanting to protect Noel, my sons and my daughter from this horror. We got everybody home except Noelle, whom we decided to leave to finish her exams. David would have to learn the devastating news over the phone. It was heartbreaking to watch as Niall and Stephen learned what had happened, and I felt so helpless that there was nothing I could do to alleviate their pain. The hurt on Noel's face as he tried to take in the horror of what had happened to his child is one of my most terrible memories of that day. Here was a father who had taken part in every moment of his children's lives, who had been involved in every stage of their growing up, who had taken them out for drives and treks in the mountains every weekend, talking to them about the wonders of nature, exploring with them old castles and cathedrals, teaching them the history of places they visited. Here was a father who had passed on to his children his love of the mountains and waterfalls, summer days and the joy of swimming and fishing in a river, who had so often brought them home, muddy and dripping wet after a day of adventure, who had so often lost patience with their squabbling in the car, threatening to throw them out and make them walk, until they all collapsed in giggles at their dad's irritation – all squabbles forgotten. Here was a man who deeply, deeply loved his children, and who now had heard that his treasured youngest son had just been cut down from the tree where his children, and he himself in his childhood, had played. I found this almost unbearable. I would have taken all his pain on myself if I had been able to. It was dreadful to watch his heart breaking like this.

Support from Neighbours and Friends

The day wore on in a haze of people coming and going; neighbours, friends and relatives bringing tray upon tray of hot and cold food; everyone crowding into the kitchen and around the table, from which neither Noel nor I had moved since morning. I remember looking at Noel and wondering how he was managing to chat about ordinary things to people. I realised that this was his way of coping with his devastation – being surrounded by people, being his usual sociable self. I recall being glad for him, however, I couldn't bring myself to enter into it. Listening, I silently screamed: 'Why are you not talking about Alan? How can you all talk about ordinary things when you can see what has happened?' I remember the rage I felt when some well-meaning soul launched into a story of how sad they had felt at the funeral of some distant cousin or other. I was screaming inside again: 'I don't *care* about your cousin's funeral or the gruesome details of his terminal disease, or how his widow crumbled in a devastated heap on her way out of the church. Why can't you just shut up and either talk about my son or *go!*'

I wanted to run, to escape from the incessant chatter, to be alone with what had happened, to process this nightmare in my mind, and yet I was afraid to be without all these people, afraid to be left alone with the reality of what had happened. This is all I remember of a day that no parent should ever have to go through. Noel and Niall went to the hospital where Alan had been taken for an autopsy. Noel said that this was one of the more traumatic events of that time, knowing that Alan was there and not being allowed to see him, because they were about to begin the post-mortem examination. He hated the thought of what was about to happen to Alan's body and assured the person dealing with the formalities that Alan was not a heavy drinker, nor a smoker or any type of drug abuser, hoping that they would take his word for it and not carry out the autopsy. However, this is a legal requirement in all suicide cases. The post-mortem examination revealed that, in fact, Alan had quite a high level of alcohol in his blood at the time of death.

Glenealy

Some time between the Friday that Alan died and the removal of his body to the church on the following Tuesday, I felt strongly drawn to Glenealy, Co. Wicklow, where my grandparents and my father are buried. My godmother is there too, but my desire was to go to my beloved grandad and my dad, two people whom I had truly loved and whose love for me I had always been certain of. Noel drove me and I remember I had my eyes closed to block out everything around me. I couldn't bear to see life outside going on as usual. I felt safe in my own interior world. I was aware that Noel was coping better than I was by facing reality head-on, while I wanted to run from it. We didn't speak much and, soon after we began the journey, I silently pleaded: 'Where are you, Alan?' and had an immediate impression of Alan's face, radiant and smiling at me, saying: 'It's deadly, Mam!' This lasted for just an instant and then it was gone. 'Deadly' is not a word that I use, and six years later the memory of that couple of seconds is as vivid as when it happened. I make no judgement on this – I am aware that intensity of emotion can cause a person to conjure up all sorts of things – but this was real to me that day and it brought me some comfort.

When we arrived at the old graveyard overlooking the village of Glenealy, I sat down on the stone edge of the grave and looked down at the little village church, and behind that the 'fairy hill', which was inhabited – according to the stories my father told us when we were children – by mischievous leprechauns whose trickery on the local people was the subject of these exciting tales. This came into my mind that day, along with other sweet recollections of my childhood in this beautiful place. It was so peaceful here now, so tranquil, like a balm gently soothing the hurt in my soul. I remember wishing I could stay there forever and not have to return to the heartbreak and chaos from which I had been given brief respite. I wished that Noel, my children and I could stop the clock – and the pain – right here.

Very softly, into my mind came my father's voice: 'That's the stuff! That's the stuff!' Then my grandfather's voice saying: 'Carol Anne, Carol Anne'. Over and over these words were repeated, all very softly, all seeming absolutely real. 'That's the stuff' was always my father's way of saying, 'Good for you!' or 'Well done!' when we did well at something. My grandad was the only one in our family who had always called me by my full name, and it always sounded like 'Carlann' in his Wicklow accent. The memory of hearing those two distinct voices, soft and loving, stay with me to this day. Again, I make no judgement; if hearing these voices was a product of my intense grief and desire for consolation, so be it. If there truly is such a thing as the spiritual presence of our loved ones after death, I thank God. However, the fact that all this happened within a couple of hours on the same day, that each seemed to speak in his own voice, that each brought me – and continues to bring me – solace, and that this has stayed fresh in my memory for six years, makes me wonder ... In my fear of being overwhelmed by the loss of Alan, in my trying to cope with the horror of his suicide, was my dad trying to tell me that I would survive, that I would be okay? Whatever the explanation, it brought me comfort in the aftermath of Alan's death.

Chapter 2

Memories

'There are two parties to the suffering that death inflicts; and, in the apportionment of this suffering, the survivors take the brunt.'

Arnold Toynbee

I was reluctant at first to ask my family to revisit the initial acute pain of losing Alan for the purpose of this book and I am grateful that they responded so readily. I feel that this brings a broader perspective to the account of Alan's suicide and may be of help to the reader in understanding just how horrific it is to lose a loved one in this way. Noel, although a sociable and chatty person, is private about deeper feelings and declined to put anything into writing. Stephen, now living so far away from us in the Philippines, found even the thought of reviving the memory of those events too painful at the time, however, he has contributed a reflection in the last chapter of the book, which was written a few months later. Noelle, David, Niall and Alan's godmother, Frances, to whom he was very close, provide their reflections here, as does Íde, who was Alan's girlfriend and confidante at the time.

Noelle

The day that Alan died was the last day of my Junior Cert. mock exams. I walked out of my Home Economics exam feeling elated, to be met by a teacher telling me that my dad was here to pick me up. Thinking nothing of it, I offered my friends, Deirdre and Alannah, a lift with us. In the reception area I was met by a swollen-eyed Niall who told my friends that unfortunately they could not come with us. Immediately, I asked Niall who had died – I guessed Mum first, then Nana. Niall didn't answer at once and we got into the car where Dad was looking heartbroken. Terrified, I asked again, and Dad said that Alan had had an accident. 'On his moped?' I asked, 'Is he okay?' Dad replied with something along the lines of, 'He took his own life'. Naturally, I burst into tears, but I remember feeling angry from the very beginning. An accident? That was hardly an accident! Having just been told a couple of weeks before by Alan's girlfriend that he had depression, I already felt left out of the family loop. Now I was being told that he had had an accident, before being told the truth of what had happened. Being so young, I felt isolated. In a single seat in the front of the car, crying into my own arms, having just lost my brother to an illness that I had never been given the chance to understand while he was alive, I was filled with rage.

I don't remember much of the journey home. Mum was in bits. I don't remember seeing Steve. I rang my friend Deirdre and went to stay with her, sitting in silence while she went about her business, comforting me when I had a bout of crying. I began writing poems about Alan's death that day, and reading them now I can still experience the immense sense of loss of my brother, seven years older than me, but closest in age, who looked after me and encouraged me to be the best I could be; who helped me to become interested in music; who had played football with me, always calling me 'goalie of the week'; who used to bargain with me to do things I didn't feel like doing, but that he knew I would eventually thank him for. That day I had a sense of losing the childhood belief that everybody lived to be a hundred years old. I also lost my trust in people for a while, although I never lost my love for Alan or the belief that he is with me every day, helping me to succeed in life.

Alan's suicide is the most difficult thing I have been through, and the grief attached to it can often be emotionally and physically disabling, but after all the years since he died I can be happy for Alan. If you love someone you have got to let them go, and I had no choice but to let him go. I have also let go of the anger and the distrust and have become glad that my brother is not in pain anymore.

Soon after Alan died, I had a dream that he was in the sitting room playing the guitar. I have had similar dreams after the death of my grandad and my uncle, in which it is the time of their funeral and they are sitting in our house alone, doing what they loved to do. As with the two previous dreams, Alan asked me to go to the kitchen and get him a drink, and before I went I hugged him and told him I loved him. He hugged me and told me that he loved me too. I went to get him the drink and when I returned he had gone. These dreams actually made me happy, as in each case I got the opportunity to say goodbye. From this dream about Alan, I knew for certain that he loved me. I had another where he came into my room one night and sat me up to give me a hug. Mid-dream I woke up to find myself sitting upright with my arms outstretched. Several times I have thought I heard the sound of his football boots on the hall floor. I firmly believe that Alan watches over me as much as he always did.

Although young, I have learned so much from Alan's death. I appreciate my family and tell each of them that I love them every day. The day Alan died was the most heart-wrenching day of my life, but I keep living every day with him in my heart and with the love I had for him as strong as ever. Something made me not open my bedroom curtains that day. That and all the other little blessings in our lives make me a firm believer that Alan truly loves us also.

David

As a contribution to this book, my mother asked me if I could try to describe my emotional reaction to my youngest brother Alan's decision to end his life one cold night at the end of February 2002. This is no easy task, as I find it next to impossible to verbalise my emotions at the best of times, let alone try to put words to the most brutal and mind-wrenching event of my life so far ... because how do you describe the worst day of your life? How do you gather and construct word sequences that can possibly describe the bottomless darkness, infinite hollowness and absolute psychological mutilation when the bomb dropped that day? It's not easy ... Alan had obviously had the worst day of his life the day before, so maybe he can help me to formulate this now? We all had the worst day of our lives the day he killed himself and I'm sure we all experienced it differently, because we all had to go through it alone, just like he did.

As part of my morning work ritual as a freelance web designer, I had just made a fresh pot of coffee and settled down in front of the monitors to finish building the latest website for a client here in Denmark. The sun was shining that morning, 1 March, and Ramses the cat had assumed his usual position in an all-illuminating sunbeam that was carving across the lounge, through the background music and the smell of the coffee. It was like any other morning.

I had had a few phone calls informing me of the death of friends and relatives since 1996, but none before or since have had the destructive force of this one. It has been engraved on my heart forever. One of my brothers, Niall, called at about 9.30 in the morning; the conversation went something like this:

> Me: 'Morning Bro, how are you doing this morning?'
>
> Niall: 'Man, I'm about to louse up your day completely ... ehh ...'
>
> Me: 'Why, what's happened?'
>
> Niall: 'Alan killed himself last night ... he hung himself on the tree at the end of the garden.'

A sledgehammer hit me and it knocked me west altogether. I remember asking how the family was, what the circumstances were, the chronology of events, the practical stuff, but at the same time my body was becoming increasingly numb. When I got off the phone the room began to spin and I descended into the darkest hole I have ever been in and stayed there for weeks, months.

Over the course of that day I was dragged through the entire spectrum of dark emotions from sadness to anger, from frustration to deep sorrow. I was simultaneously sad, livid yet lucid, trying to understand but torn and bleeding and helpless, as if I had just had both of my arms wrenched off and was being pounded mercilessly with the two bleeding stumps. My predominant instinct was: 'Book a flight, book a flight, get a plane home now, I'll drive if I have to.' It seemed both rational and viable at the time.

I cannot remember if it was hours or days before I was on a plane back to Dublin, but the hours in between were torture. Telling people what had happened was stomach churning. I'm sure my family in Dublin felt that way also. My girlfriend, Merete – who is now my wife – cut in at one point to handle all of that, informing the relevant people for me so that I could focus on packing a case and keeping my head together. In Danish, the word for suicide is '*selv-mord*', which literally means 'self-murder'. I heard that word maybe thirty times that day, but it was far easier to hear Merete say it than to say it myself. Alan had murdered himself. I clearly remember a call from my other brother, Steve, later that day, which brought me to new depths of sorrow and anguish. He was ripped apart also, and was particularly adept at vocalising it. He was expressing everything that I was incapable of saying.

Landing in Dublin was an emotionally charged experience, to say the least. However, arriving at the house was like setting foot on a scorched wasteland, an apocalyptic scene or the surrealism of a Dali painting. Emotional debris was everywhere – burning people so badly damaged they could never be whole again. I have never hugged so many people at one time before, but nothing could put the flames out.

The removal and funeral were another two dark days for everyone. The second worst day ever, for everyone – the songs, *Babylon*, the cremation, all the tears and the empty eyes that couldn't cry any more. The church was packed; it was like Easter: 'St Alan's Day', I thought. He would have been impressed by the amount of people who turned up to say goodbye. I know I was, and in some weird way I was proud of him for being able to draw such a large crowd! It's bizarre the way the mind works to help us through these situations. At the removal, the condolence procession was difficult also, and looking at our mother I heard myself say aloud: 'How much more of this can she take?' Crowds of people of all ages, shapes and sizes; nice people, wholehearted and real, honestly paying their respects, but at one point it seemed like my mother was about to fall, so I made an executive decision to immediately extract her from her front row seat. Steve, Niall and I distracted people long enough for her to make her escape.

The next few days were spent watching the suicide ripple spread through everyone Alan had known. His friends calling around, the tears, the funny stories, the jokes and trying to get our heads around why he had made a decision like that; trying to fathom the pain he must have felt, the anger, loneliness, darkness, emptiness, his own personal hell in which he was entangled, which nobody could save him from, these infinitely dark emotions culminating in this final, all-obliterating action. To meet this side of Alan was not only shocking, but surprising, because he was one of the funniest and most entertaining people I have ever known.

I miss Alan a lot and often. His death has changed all of us. Whole dimensions of us as individuals and as a family have been removed forever and none of us have been the same since. We're burned and scarred.

Niall

I remember 1 March 2002 vividly. Walking to work along Baggot Street, I was thinking to myself that I was pretty content in my life at that time, and I remember that thought because thirty seconds later I got a phone call from a garda asking me to come home. I immediately assumed that something bad had happened to someone and the first person I thought of was Alan. He owned a moped at the time and we had been worried about him having an accident.

I arrived home to find several police cars outside and gardaí and detectives in the hallway. I was ushered into the kitchen by one of them, where I found my mother and father sitting at the table. 'He's gone', my mum told me, 'Alan's gone'. My dad was ashen, in total shock. I couldn't believe it. I stood there, stunned for a few moments, and then went to hug my parents. I cried with them, but part of me told myself that I would have to take some sort of responsibility for the rest of my family. Steve was beside himself. He went upstairs and saw Alan lying on the ground in the garden after he had been cut from the tree on which he had killed himself – he screamed a few times. I had never been in a situation like this before. I was watching their hearts and my own being broken.

I thought of my sister, only fifteen, in school; she would have to be told. I thought of my grandmother, aged eighty-six, who had already lost her husband and one of her sons in the previous three years. Steve came downstairs and a garda came into the kitchen and asked if one of us could identify the body. Steve and I wanted to do it, because it was unthinkable to us that Mum or Dad would have to identify their son outside the house. We were taken out to the ambulance and they lifted a sheet. Until that moment I had held out a ridiculous hope that it wouldn't be him and that it was a mistake – but it was Alan. I touched his hair and told him how much I loved him, they covered him up and Steve and I hugged each other on the steps outside the house.

I called my eldest brother, Dave, to tell him. I remember calling Alan's friends to tell them ... difficult conversations. When the gardaí left, the cut piece of rope remained hanging from the tree. The ladder used to cut him down was still in place. (Thank you, Frances, for removing them.) Taking responsibility for others was my way of storing away the horror of what had happened until I could deal with it. Later that day, sitting in the car with Dad, I felt my anger rising because it was such a waste of a life. Alan was a glorious human being, talented and kind, and I was furious that he had taken his own life.

Dad and I went to collect Noelle from school when her exams were over. She guessed something was up and asked us who had died. It will remain the most heartbreaking moment of my life when Dad told her. Only fifteen and, at that moment, part of her innocence was taken away. Being ten years older, my instinct had always been to protect her, and that was why it was so difficult for me to see this happen. Another reason I was angry with Al was that he had killed himself in plain view of my sister's window. I thank God she didn't open her curtains and see him when she got up. (That horror befell our neighbour, who saw Alan hanging from the branch in the reflection of a mirror and called the gardaí. I have often thought about the pain that this must have caused her.) But then, how can you stay angry at someone you love so much, who was in so much pain that they couldn't see the damage they would cause just in the manner in which they took their life? We went to tell my grandmother next and she was totally distraught. At eighty-six you never expect to see a grandchild pass before you.

Over the next couple of days I remember a lot of tears, mostly when my friends, the majority of whom had known Alan well, saw me for the first time since his death. I will always be grateful for their support; my anger and sorrow were certainly eased by their love.

I remember telling Alan once that if he ever killed himself it would destroy me, and it did for nearly two years as I struggled to come to terms with the absolute waste of a life that had occurred and with the pain of missing him. I loved him completely. I thought he was such an original character and as brothers we were lucky because we got on so well, shared friends, played music and socialised together. There was just eighteen months between us.

I sought hope in such sorrow and I found it eventually. I realised that we are truly all the same in a certain respect and a great compassion arose out of that. I realised that if circumstances had been different, it could have been me hanging from that branch. Understanding this means that I can no longer be angry with Alan for what he did, or feel any guilt or remorse for any part I think I may have had in his death.

I treasure my last memory of Alan alive. He had been at the pub with his friends and came in around midnight. I was on my way to bed and stopped to play with one of Alan's cats on the stairs. Alan walked in and we exchanged a few words and I said goodnight with affection. I'm glad that the last words he heard in this life were loving words. I was the last person to see him alive, because a short time later that night he was dead.

To finish, there are two things worth noting. One, I believe that for a couple of weeks after he died, I sensed Alan's presence several times. This was a palpable feeling and I also had several dreams in which he spoke to me about what had happened. Two, I believe that one day, in some form, I will be with him once again and I will have the opportunity to love him even more next time – and next time I will watch over him a lot more carefully.

Frances

At 12.40 on the morning of 1 March 2002, I was awakened from sleep with the sensation of choking. I couldn't catch a breath. The experience was so real and so frightening that I told my colleagues in work about it the next morning. A couple of hours into my working day my phone rang and it was Carol, asking if I could come up to her house. I asked why and she replied that it didn't matter and she was sorry for bothering me. I put the phone down and started to shake. I knew this had to be serious, because Carol would never ring asking me to leave work unless something terrible had happened. I rang her back and a garda answered, asking me to come to the house. I immediately thought of Alan. Little did I know then that he had died at 12.40 that morning. Shaking, feeling really nervous, I rang my husband, Danny, told him what the garda had said and asked him to meet me so that we could go together.

In the car, I remember sitting in silence, afraid of the horror that I knew was about to unfold. I saw the police cars and the ambulance. The rest became so surreal: walking past the two gardaí in the hallway into the kitchen, where the faces of everyone told their own story. Noel was sitting at the kitchen table, his eyes swollen and red from crying. Carol hugged me and said, 'Alan's gone'. I went to Niall and put my arms around him and shouted over and over again, 'Oh God, no!' I kept repeating this as if it would make all this go away. I could see Danny standing by the sink looking totally distraught, with no words to say, but a look of horror on his face.

It became even more real when I learned that Alan's body had not been removed, but was still lying in the garden. One part of me wanted to go out to him, to comfort him, and the other part was so frightened to see the stillness of his body, the life gone from this unique person, whom down the years I had watched, admired and loved for his humour, his energy and his passion for life. So many emotions were running through me in every direction: poor Carol, poor Noel, poor Stephen, Niall, David and Noelle. How would they ever come to terms with this? I felt so helpless, so powerless, that horrible sick feeling that churns away deep within.

I could hear the screams of Stephen upstairs, a sound I never want to hear again, like a wounded animal, unable to cope with the pain ... screeching, kicking, wanting to escape, but having nowhere to escape to. They would have to let Noelle know. She was still at school. My heart went out to them. I could imagine her sitting in school, oblivious to the devastation at home. She was about to hear the most shattering news of her young life and there was nothing any of us could do to stop it.

After they had taken Alan away to Loughlinstown Hospital for a post-mortem, the hospital where he and my daughter had been born within six months of one another twenty-two years earlier, I looked out of the living room window at the garden and saw the ladder by the tree and part of the rope still remaining. I had to get it down before Noelle saw it. I ran into the kitchen, grabbed a carving knife, ran down the garden, climbed the ladder and started to hack away at the rope. It was very strong and it took all the energy I could muster, but the strength came from every emotion in my body. I held the rope in my hand and threw it as far as I could, throwing with it all my hurt, anger, sadness and frustration. Then I felt drained.

I then had the difficult task of phoning my daughter, Danielle. I knew she would be devastated, as she and Alan went back a long way. She loved him to bits. They had grown up together. When I told her, she didn't want to come out to the house, but wanted to be alone to absorb the full horror of what had happened and, I'm sure, to cry the tears which I knew would flow in abundance.

The next couple of days went by in a blur of people coming and going, everyone needing everyone. Some of us had to be distracted: we needed to talk about Alan, laugh about Alan, anything to keep us from dwelling on the awfulness of what had happened; emotions were so raw.

After the funeral, Carol went into her own little world, listening to music and arranging and rearranging the hundreds of flowers that had been sent. It appeared to me that she was in a spiritual place, a quiet place where she and her beloved son were together, full of sadness and love, but strangely at peace.

Íde

The Thursday evening of Alan's death I rang him from work for a chat, but midway through our conversation I got called away, so I hurriedly said goodbye to him and told him I loved him. That was the last time I spoke to him. We had spent the Wednesday evening together, and he was preparing his CV, which I took as an indication that he was doing well. We spent the rest of the evening curled up on the sofa with a movie and a take away, blissfully unaware of what lay ahead.

On Friday morning I woke up to a phone call. I was working as a veterinary nurse at the time and being on the late shift I was able to sleep in. From the number that flashed on the screen of my phone I was expecting to hear Alan's voice at the other end of the line. Instead, it was a garda who told me I needed to get to Alan's home as soon as possible. Naturally, I asked what was wrong, but the garda wouldn't give me any details. All he seemed to be concerned with was how I was going to get to my destination and suggested that I call someone to drive me. I knew right then what had happened. I called my sister, but she was working and couldn't come to the phone. I then called her boyfriend who came to collect me and tried to reassure me that there was some simple explanation for all this. But I knew there wasn't. As soon as Alan's mom opened the door, no words needed to be spoken.

I don't remember much of the day from that point onwards. I know I collapsed in a heap crying when my worst nightmare was confirmed, but that's all – just pain from then onwards and then guilt. I was never really angry with Alan; after all, he had warned me that he intended to take his life. I was angry with others, but mostly angry with myself.

I remember certain times of those horrible days after his death. Seeing him in his coffin is a moment that has been imprinted on my mind forever. The rest of the time is a blur, full of mixed up memories. What hurts and saddens me most is thinking of how alone he must have felt in his final moments. Losing Alan marked the worst time in my life, but I try to focus on our times together, just the two of us. He made me laugh, made me happy, made me worry and cry; our relationship was intense and unforgettable.

I sometimes wonder what my life would have been like if I had never met and fallen in love with Alan and I come up with nothing. I'm a better person for having known him, and in that respect I have no regrets.

Honesty is the Best Policy
These stories reflect the anguish that is felt at the loss of a brother, cousin and boyfriend. I can see from what Noelle has written that by trying to protect her from Alan's illness we treated her very unjustly. She saw it as deception and it is no wonder she felt betrayed by us. This led to a breakdown in her trust of her parents and caused her to feel iso-

lated and alone. She eventually came to understand that we were trying to protect her, however, it could have caused lasting damage to her relationship with us and it only served to add to her anguish at the time. This has taught me the importance of being open and honest about family issues; that this is a far more healthy way of dealing with things.

Even if it is not to be written for publication, I feel that it is good for anyone who is bereaved to write down their thoughts and feelings. If this is done frequently, we can look back over it from time to time and see that we are, in fact, moving on with life, even when we feel that we will never recover from the heartache of our loss. Of course, journaling cannot take the place of being able to talk out one's feelings, preferably with a person who has been trained to listen actively without judging or giving advice, but even to unburden oneself to a trusted friend who is a good listener can be therapeutic. When Alan was feeling down and wouldn't agree to go for professional help, I suggested that he write down his thoughts and feelings, and I am so glad he did this because it provided me with valuable insight and understanding about the extremely disabling and unpredictable nature of even a mild form of bipolar disorder.

Chapter 3

'Under the Gaze of God'

'When believers pray under the gaze of God, there is standing with them the angel of prayer.'

Tertullian

Dread

On the Monday following Alan's death, his body was released to the undertakers, who requested that we bring some clothes to dress him in. We chose his favourite blue flowered shirt and 'good' jeans (as opposed to the many pairs he owned which had rips in them, a fashion statement at the time). Alan had been very particular about his appearance and we needed to get this right! I think he would have been pleased with our choice of outfit; he had always looked lovely in it.

I desperately did not want to go through the whole nightmare of Alan's funeral and the prospect of having to endure the two days filled me with real terror. I wanted it all to pass by and, no matter how family and friends tried to persuade me, I said that I would not go. My family didn't need me there, I reasoned to myself, everyone had plenty of support. No one would know whether I was there or not, and if they did, what did it matter? I was not aware at that time that I was being utterly self-centred about this, and I could not understand why I couldn't just be left alone to do what I wanted to do, which was to hide from the ordeal of seeing my dead child in a coffin and having to talk to people. Why were they all so insistent that I be there? My Alan was dead and no rite or ritual could bring him back. That's all that mattered. If it were to be with God, that was crazy! I didn't need to go through torture to be with God; God was here with me; God can't go anywhere and I didn't need to go anywhere to be with God. Could they not see that?

The value of gathering in the church with family, friends and the wider community, even the power of communal prayer, in which I have a deep belief, was lost on me at that time. The consolation that this brings to a grieving family – that it would bring to me and my family – never crossed my mind. At the funerals of my father and brother I had been full of gratitude for the support that neighbours and friends had shown to our family, and had seen this as a very important and healing element in our grieving process, but now my reasoning was so skewed and so self-referred that this was forgotten. My instinct was to survive this horror and staying away from people would be my way of surviving.

Somebody in the family finally penetrated this irrational thinking and when the cars came to take us to the funeral home I reluctantly went along. I remember that in the car a part of me wanted to reach out to Noel and my children to try to comfort them, but I was incapable, so intent was I on getting through this nightmare. I recall thinking that at least one can wake up from a nightmare and all is right again. From this there would be no waking up. I remember, as we drove to see Alan, feeling totally trapped.

Removal

At the funeral home, we were taken into a room where we would see our son for the last time. I went to where Alan lay, all life gone from his face, dark hair, eyebrows and lashes in stark contrast to the pallor of his skin. His face, though skillfully embalmed, was an inanimate face, every vestige of expression gone, leaving no clue for me as to how he had felt in his final moments. This face that had been so mobile, the green eyes so expressive of emotion – happy, mischievous, anxious, sad. This was a shell, yet this was my Alan, my noisy, gifted, creative, outrageous Alan. My beautiful boy whom for twenty-two years had brought into our lives fun and joy, worry and tears, and had inspired in all of us a depth of love that we can only be grateful to have experienced; who would never laugh again, would never cry again, the husky voice that would never sing again, that would never call, 'Where's Mam?' again when he came in from school or work. The words of love now pouring from me as I caressed his face bounced off this cold, impenetrable shell and back to me. They closed the coffin. Alan had gone from us ... our darkest hour. The pain cannot be described, yet it had to be lived.

We were taken to the church where what appeared to me to be hundreds of people waited outside to accompany us in. Watching my sons carry their brother's coffin into the church was excruciating. Parents before us, and parents since, have been through this experience; only they know what it feels like to watch. When everybody had settled and there was silence, the soft strains of 'Whispering Hope' began to fill the hush. My friends, Marie and Conor, gifted singers and guitarists who had been with me the previous night arranging the music and readings for the Mass, had decided, unknown to me, to contribute this song to the removal proceedings and it was a beautiful addition to that ceremony. Prayers were said and I remember crowds of people coming up to where we were in the church to offer their condolence. This again is very important to the bereaved family – a show of concern and solidarity in their grief – and I was amazed and extremely grateful to the people who queued patiently to offer their sympathy. I could only stay for a while, though, before I began to feel dizzy and someone took me out of the church.

Funeral

The following day was the funeral Mass, the chief celebrant of which was Fr Michael, who had served as a curate in our parish and had moved a couple of years previous to be parish priest in another area. We knew Fr Michael as a good friend of the family and were delighted to have him celebrate Alan's funeral Mass, as Alan had been part of the church folk group while Fr Michael had been in our parish. I still remember the silence that descended on the church after the entrance hymn had been sung. The celebrant came down the steps and stood facing the large congregation. 'Under the gaze of God', he said quietly, pausing, and again, 'Under the gaze of God'. These words seemed to penetrate the confusion and chaos in my spirit, and I experienced a deep sense of peace, a sense of unity with every person in the crowded church. I felt that a greater Presence was enveloping all of us in a steady, gentle, loving gaze. Fr Michael was in no hurry to get on with the Mass and allowed the silence to speak, allowed this graced moment to unfold.

That is a memory that stays with me to this day, and I see it as a moment in which the consoling presence of God was revealed to a grieving community. A lot of people afterwards spoke to me of the atmosphere of love that was in the church that morning. For the duration of the Mass I could feel a sense of peace that I had not known since Alan's death. This lasted only until the Mass was over, but in the following months I was to remember it many times.

Reflecting on those two days and on the moments of solace experienced on both of them, I am glad that I was persuaded to be there, reluctant as I had been to go. Having felt that I would not be able to cope with all the people, I have since been extremely grateful and appreciative of the support and the compassion shown to us by our community. This indeed is a vital healing element of the grieving process.

The Final Stage of Saying Goodbye

From the church we went to the crematorium in Mount Jerome cemetery, the last stage of this awful couple of days for which our sons had been given the task of organising the music. They chose a selection of songs by David Gray, one of Alan's favourite musicians. Our house had often been filled with the sound of Alan singing 'Babylon', a passionate song that he had loved. Now, as the song was playing, our children and Alan's friends all held hands and sang the chorus from their hearts, singing at the tops of their voices, singing out their grief at the loss of their beloved brother and friend. During the short ceremony, Fr Michael asked Noel and I to approach Alan's coffin and bless it with holy water, to symbolise that just as we had taken him to the church for Baptism with water, we were now taking him to the church to be sent back to God with water. It was a beautiful moment, but only in retrospect. The curtains drew slowly around the coffin and the light shining through them grew gradually dimmer – and then we could see no more. Writing this now, my heart is sore and the memory of the desolation I felt then is still fresh.

As the years have gone by and the tide of memory has receded, some significant moments of consolation during those two days stay with me, moments of which I saw the significance only afterwards. On the day of the removal of Alan's body to the church, Noel went to a local men's outfitters to buy some new clothes for the funeral. The proprietor of the shop is also called Noel and in the course of conversation it emerged that one year previous, almost to the day, he, too, had lost his twenty-one-year-old son, also called Alan, to suicide. Like our Alan, this man's son had been diagnosed with depression, appeared to have had everything going for him in his life and was into sports and fitness – an almost identical set of circumstances to our son's. Noel found consolation in this encounter with someone who could identify with what he was going through and has since been comforted by their occasional chats. Angels come in all guises.

Another significant event of the time was learning about the 'grieving candle'. During the funeral Mass, a friend of ours went to the altar, lit a special candle and explained to the congregation that this candle would be given to our family, so that it could be lit for a certain period of time each day – a time during which we could focus on remembering Alan, pray for him or think about his life. Then the candle is extinguished and lit again the next day, and so on until the candle is used up, by which time the initial acute grief will have subsided. Every morning I would set aside a half an hour when I was alone to focus on Alan and remember every detail of what had happened. This was helpful in clarifying the events for me and in helping to keep me grounded in reality. The confusion and sense of unreality at that time meant that my mind could go around in circles and this focussing time, though initially extremely painful, was of great benefit to me in facing up to what had happened.

I recall on one occasion imagining the final few moments of Alan's life: I was with him as he came in and said goodnight to Niall; as he opened the patio door and went out; as he collected the ladder and blue nylon rope from the shed and walked to the tree at the bottom of the garden; with him as he climbed the ladder and put the rope around his neck; with him in his last moment. I was with him in my imagination, but the excruciating guilt that I was not physically there for my child in his darkest moment I could not erase. I thought I would lose my own grip on life at that time, which is why I needed to face this reality. However, if I am honest, I could also have wished to punish myself for what I perceived as my neglect of him.

A third event that had a positive impact on me and that was truly life-changing was when I was advised to 'live in the now'. It was in May of that year, three months after Alan died, that my friends, Marie and Conor, suggested I go along with them to a 'healing' Mass in Kildare. They felt that it would be good for me, and I would have agreed to anything at that time that I thought would bring me some help in the daily struggle to get used to the altered life that we were now forced to lead without Alan. The theme that emerged in the Mass was the importance of living in the present moment, because that is the only reality we have, the future being illusory. I was very moved by this and later when I spoke to the celebrant, a person whom I had always admired for his wisdom, about what had occurred in my life, he said only, 'Try to live in the now'. I began to train myself to do this and gradually learned to be conscious of living neither in the past nor in the future, but being fully present to life as it is at this moment. This mindfulness is difficult to achieve and requires much self-discipline, but, fortunately, when I fall away from it I can just take my mind back to the present moment and try again. This way of living not only helped me to cope with my grief back then, but continues to be part of the way I try to live now. I find that where I used to worry about the future and used to feel anxious about things, I have become much more at ease with life. Added to this is the sense that life has thrown at me the very worst that can ever happen and I have survived. Nothing will ever be as difficult as the struggle to go on living after Alan's suicide.

Chapter 4

A Changed Life

'Suicide is a death like no other, and those that are left behind to struggle with it must confront a pain like no other. Suicide is not a deathbed gathering; it rips apart lives and beliefs, and it sets its survivors on a prolonged and devastating journey.'

Kay Redfield Jamison

A Hole in the Soul

Someone described the scar that suicide survivors carry with them as 'a hole in the soul'– an apt description. It is seven years since Alan's death and only after months of therapy last year did I feel that I was truly able to move on with my life. In the aftermath of the death we move on because we have no choice; life moves on and we are carried with it. It is as if we are being transported by a current, yet struggling against it.

Suicide Survivors

There was a time when I would have seen 'suicide survivors' as those who had survived their own suicide attempt, however, I can now see how the term can rightly be used in referring to those of us who have survived the loss of a dearly loved member of our family to suicide. We as suicide survivors have received an emotional shock, we feel grief, guilt, remorse and rejection; we have had our relationship with our lost loved one suddenly destroyed. In my experience so far, survival of trauma such as this is a long and circuitous journey; a process filled with reminders, refreshed pain and hopelessness – one step forward and two steps backward. A song, a smell, a place or a person can reawaken the devastation of the initial grief and one can feel that it will never get any better.

When Elizabeth Kübler-Ross wrote her book *On Death and Dying* in 1969, grief was thought to be a process that happened in a systematic manner. First there would be denial ('this is not happening to me'), then anger ('why is this happening to me?'), followed by bargaining ('I'll be a better person if ...'), depression ('I give up') and acceptance ('I am ready for what's ahead of me'). Only more recently have we learned that many people do not go through all of these phases and that these phases can and do occur in different orders. Grieving is now beginning to be recognised as mainly an individual process, and hopefully therapists are beginning to be less inclined to follow a prescribed set of stages when engaging with clients in bereavement counselling.

To me, surviving suicide, especially the suicide of one's child, is not merely going through an ordered process, then picking up the threads of life and eventually moving on; rather, it is something that can at times seem impossible to move on from. Studies have shown that bereavement by suicide does not differ from the impact of other sudden death. However, the grief following a suicide can be compounded by feelings of guilt, self-blame and rejection. Stigmatisation and shame can also become part of the mix, all of which can make coping with the loss extremely difficult.

I remember that when we came back from Alan's funeral there was a letter waiting for me in the hall. A friend had written of her admiration for Stephen and Niall in openly addressing the manner of Alan's death during the funeral mass. She wrote that she had lost her brother in the same way, but that her parents would never permit it to be mentioned publicly and that this had had a negative impact on the family as a unit. I admired her courage and openness in writing the letter and at the same time felt sad that her family had lived with this sense of shame.

Guilt

Guilt made a huge dent in my sense of self-worth when Alan died. I wanted to be strong for my children, but found it impossible. I felt a failure as a mother. Not alone had I failed in not preventing Alan's death, but now I was letting the rest of my children down by not being able to ease their pain. The most difficult task of parenting is to hold our children close and keep them safe, while at the same time letting them go. In my distorted view at that time, I had failed to keep Alan safe and now I was failing my other children, as I was sure I had failed them in so many ways throughout their lives. I often recalled the many times I had been angry with my children and raised my voice at them in frustration. If only I had been more patient. I remembered the many times I had been too busy with my own concerns to give them my undivided attention. If only I had kept my priorities right. If only I had been a better mother ... if only ... if only ... I was driving myself mad with irrational guilt that at the time made perfect sense to me. In hindsight, the healthy thing to do would have been to talk these feelings out with a trained therapist, who could be objective in the situation and who could point out to me that no parent is perfect and that I had been an adequate mother, which is all any parent can hope to be.

Choice

The issue of choice also preoccupied me in a negative way. Suicide is an individual choice and no one was to blame for Alan's choice to end his life. Alan had chosen to leave us, knowing how deeply he was loved. How could we not feel abandoned and rejected? Was his family not worth living for? I can see that for a family bereaved by suicide, the fact that a loved one's death appears to involve an element of choice can raise painful questions that a death from a natural or accidental cause does not. We can be plagued with the 'why' of suicide for a long time. All of the family went through this painful questioning, trying to make some sense of Alan's death.

Blame

I have learned through experience that it can be a risk to the family as a unit to focus too much on trying to get into the mind of the suicidal person at the time of their decision to stop living. I found myself looking at each of us and trying to pinpoint a certain disagreement, a certain situation in which there was conflict, a certain family member with whom Alan was resentful or angry, including myself. This only served to make me look at myself and my family in a suspicious way, which served no purpose at all and was potentially destructive to relationships within the family. No matter how many reasons one comes up with, it is impossible to know the thoughts of the deceased. In our desire to neatly tie up the ends of the 'why' question, it is all too easy for family members to look at one another and lay blame on a particular event, a particular personality clash or the deceased's anger towards a particular person.

The person who has died may also have been trying to make sense of their own depression and self-disgust and may have used a family member as a scapegoat in order to do this, laying blame on the person for perceived wrongs.

Blaming can be a way of dealing with grief, but it is a counter-productive way of dealing, giving only temporary relief and causing damage to relationships within the family at a time when they need each other most. I have learned that there is no one person or one event that causes a person to take their own life; that the whole truth of a suicide mostly dies with the person who has completed the suicide.

Anxiety

Another aspect of that intense grief was worrying about my own safety and that of my family. Identification with someone who has taken their life can be extremely threatening to a family's sense of security. Research has shown that those bereaved by suicide may suffer more anxiety than those bereaved in other ways, and they may be more vulnerable to suicidal feelings of their own. Although I had never before contemplated suicide, one of my biggest fears following Alan's death was not only that another of my children would die in a similar way, but that I would lose control and become so overwhelmed by the power of my emotions that I would end my life also. Within a couple of weeks after Alan's death I heard of two other young men in our locality who had completed suicide, and this contributed to the feeling of insecurity in my world. Something to which I had not previously given much thought had suddenly become a reality, a new part of my life.

I remember waking one morning to a now familiar nightmare and thinking that it would be easy to end this torment by following Alan, and I could actually see the point in what he had done. This feeling was real and very strong, and the only thing that stopped me was the thought of what it would do to my already grieving family, so I kept it to myself. Looking back now, I was in a depressed and vulnerable state, and again took a risk in not seeking professional help where I could express these feelings in safety and where I would have learned that suicidal ideation is a common reaction among suicide survivors.

My son, Stephen, who now lives in the Philippines with his wife and two baby daughters, told me in a recent phone conversation about having similar feelings at that time: 'Psychically, or spiritually, Alan's death hurt me so much that at times I also wanted to leave. My desire was to die. One time crossing O'Connell Bridge I had an impulse to jump into the river and end the pain, but I wouldn't allow myself to entertain the thought. My mind wouldn't entertain the thought but my heart wanted to follow Alan, it was so painful to be without him.'

Fear

While outwardly I appeared to be coping, inside I was becoming more and more terrified. I was frightened of everything: of being in the world, the prospect of something equally horrendous happening to my family and me, my own sadness and the total unpredictability of this destructive force, which could rip asunder all that was familiar. Terror could immobilise me for hours at a time. I experienced panic attacks and a sick feeling in my stomach when the stress built up and could only be relieved when I howled my grief into a towel to muffle the sound from my family. Every time I cried the nausea and panic would subside for another while. I have since learned that tears contain stress hormones and that when we shed tears we release stress. This certainly proved to be true. I had never known desolation like this. I remember trying to describe it to someone at the time and the only words I could say were 'something is gone from my womb'. Something was missing from me on a level more profound than I could express in words. When my father and my brother died I had felt extremely sad and still miss them to this day because I loved both of them deeply, but the feeling of loss was little in comparison to the brutal assault on my body and mind in the days and weeks following Alan's death.

I recall going into Alan's bedroom a couple of days after his death and standing there, looking around at his things. I picked up a shirt that he had worn recently and I could pick up his familiar scent. I came across his football boots, the grass and mud on them still fresh from his last football practice, and this brought on a fresh wave of almost unbearable grief. For weeks after he died I was finding photographs or notes he had written when he was trying to exorcise the demon of depression from his mind. Reading them gave me some insight into the way he had been feeling in his final months and weeks, it broke my heart to think that Alan's cheerful exterior had concealed feelings of such confusion, deep sadness and despair. Reading what he had written also showed how strongly he had tried to fight the ruinous illness that is depression by writing down his thoughts and feelings in the hope that he could understand why this had visited him.

Giving One Another Space to Grieve

As people's needs are different, so too are their ways of expressing their feelings. Each of us in the family needed room and understanding to express what we were feeling in our own way. The worst thing at that time would have been to 'walk on eggshells' around one another, although initially that did happen, which is normal under the circumstances. I know that at times I was conscious of putting on a brave face for the rest of the family and this was exhausting and lonely. I remember being half afraid to bring up Alan's name for fear of upsetting the others. Noel went back to work quite soon after Alan's death in an effort to regain some sense of normality. I remember feeling relieved at this, firstly because I knew that he would feel happier to be out of the house and distracted from the acute pain because of his work; secondly, it relieved me of the worry that he wasn't talking much about Alan's death. I knew that this was because he did not want to upset the rest of us, so by going back to work he would be free to talk to colleagues about it.

As the rest of the family went about the business of getting back to work and school, I felt a huge sense of relief, as it was the first opportunity I had to be alone to try to come to terms with the reality of losing Alan in my own way. Some people can dread being left alone without the distraction of family, and others will identify with my need for time on my own – each of us is different. Noel hated to be alone at that time, while I craved solitude.

Each of us bore a different relationship with Alan and it was only when we accepted and respected these differences that we were able to allow each other to grieve in our own way. This is not to say that we all sat down and deliberated on how our relationship with Alan differed, but it was more of a tacit shift in our tolerance of one another's individual way of grieving.

Importance of Dealing with Feelings
In retrospect, I can see that there is danger in putting feelings of grief on hold until some vague time in the future

when the opportunity presents itself to experience them. Several times I put away important feelings, meaning to deal with them at a later time, but did not make a definite appointment with myself to process what I had stored away. Only with the help of a skilled and patient therapist five years after Alan's death was I able to revive and reflect on them. These powerful feelings can become buried within our psyche and can cause immense damage to our personality, affecting not only our mentality, but also our behaviour. Now, if I find myself in a situation where I need to put strong personal feelings on the 'back burner', I make a conscious decision to process them at a time later that day and make sure I stick to my decision. I make time to be alone and to reflect on the feelings, to allow them to resurface, to sit with them and try to discover what they are saying to me. Our feelings, if forced out of our conscious mind, are capable of becoming powerfully destructive, affecting mind and body in the future. These feelings deserve our respect and attention, even if it cannot be immediate. I have found this practice really helpful, especially given the huge range of emotions that are experienced when one is on the journey through grief.

Grieving in Adolescence

As I mentioned earlier, my daughter, Noelle, was fifteen when Alan died, and because I was so mentally and emotionally immobilised by Alan's death, it was a blessing to me that the teaching staff and counsellor at her school were so considerate and helpful to her. Her sessions with the counsellor were of real benefit to her and every one of her teachers showed great sensitivity to her situation. I have immense admiration for Noelle, because she was due to sit her Junior Cert. exams the following June, and while many young people, understandably, would have allowed their grades to fall, Noelle remembered Alan's encouragement to her to work hard in school. She vowed to study hard and to do well in her exams and she dedicated all that hard work to Alan. She did very well and we were all so proud of her. Despite all the trauma and the pain she experienced at such a young age – or maybe because of it – Noelle has grown into a sensitive, compassionate and lovely young woman, whose desire is to help others who are going through emotional pain.

It may be worthwhile at this point to reflect on how the grieving process for adolescents can differ from that of adults. Like adults, an adolescent experiences a broad range of emotional and physical reactions after losing someone significant. The archetypal experience of adolescence is the death of one's childhood and the birth of the adult self. This transition is complex and involves its own grief, because it is bereavement in its own right. When this grieving – whether conscious or unconscious – is compounded with the grief attached to the loss of a sibling by suicide, the adolescent is surely on a very rocky journey. While I worried about all my children at that time, I was particularly concerned about how Noelle would handle the loss of Alan and what long-term effect it would have on her, because she was at such a vulnerable stage in her life. I was acutely aware that I was not capable of being fully present to my children and I was afraid that this would cause further pain for Noelle and double the sense of rejection.

Helpful Responses to Grief

Like negotiating the stages of adolescence, there is no 'correct' way for the adolescent to grieve and each experience is unique and individual. There are, however, helpful and unhelpful ways to grieve. Some of the helpful ways for a young person to grieve – indeed, for all of us to grieve – would be to confide in trusted friends about feelings, try to express feelings through art or music, maybe write a poem or a song, keep a journal or diary about life without the loved one and the feelings of loss associated with it. It is most important to express emotion rather than hold it inside. Noelle expressed her grief through poetry and music. She started to teach herself how to play the guitar in memory of Alan, who loved his guitar, and she is a very good player now.

Unhelpful Responses

Some of the unhelpful grief responses, which could have long-term negative consequences, would be alcohol and other substance abuse, reckless sexual activity, antisocial behaviour and withdrawal from social activities. This could also apply to adults, however, I believe that adolescents, having their own grieving process already going on as part of growing into adulthood, can be much more vulnerable to these responses.

No Set Formula for Grieving

There is no formula for working through grief after bereavement by suicide. Each individual affected by it can only stumble through the first weeks and months, trying to make sense of their loss, while coping with feelings of guilt, depression, sometimes shame and self-blame. If I were at the beginning of the journey through the grieving process again, I would be a lot gentler with myself: I would not beat myself up trying to make sense of why Alan took his life and I would not try to hold on to my guilt, believing that I deserve to be punished for my child's death. I know now that nothing can be gained by this. Suicide is self-chosen and self-inflicted and there will always be unanswered and unanswerable questions. This is all in hindsight, however, and we all know how clear our vision can be from there! In my experience, the first glimmer of healing came when I began to accept that I may never know the answer to the 'why' of Alan's suicide. This acceptance took much time and energy, but it did eventually allow me to move on towards healing.

The Urge to Help Other Young People

A few months after Alan's death I experienced an urge to tell my story to young people in the hope that those who were experiencing depression and those who felt that life was not worth living would stop and think before destroying themselves. I felt that if they saw the consequence of suicide through the eyes of a bereaved mother it would give them some idea of the anguish experienced by those who are left behind and who have to try to overcome pain and grief and try to rebuild a life in the absence of their beloved child. I wanted to let young people – especially young men – know that depression is a very common and treatable illness, and that it is not a sign of weakness to seek help. I wanted to let them know about Alan's reluctance to seek medical help and the tragic impact that this had on his life and the lives of his family and friends. I have spoken about suicide and the features and management of depression in many schools throughout the country since then and I continue to do so. The feedback that I receive from students and school staff following these talks is invariably positive, and I know that hearing Alan's story has lead some young people to seek help in crisis. My hope is that talking openly about mental illness will help to remove the stigma that is attached to it, at least among the young people to whom I speak.

Chapter 5

The Dark Cloud of Depression

'Our Child'

by Alan Milton

There is a time in everybody's life when they must
look deep inside
And they will see the child that must be freed.

If this world were a little friendlier, we could all
live in peace
If we weren't so quick to grow up we could see
what we need.
If we were like children, playing in a park
If we were like children, frightened of the dark
If we were like children, who aren't sure what to do
Maybe we could all be happy
Like a child without a clue, seeing everything as new,
And with a child's eyes we could all love true.

What happened to that child inside, the one full of love?
What happened to that child inside, the one full
of happiness?
What happened to that child inside?
When things were simpler?
What happened to that child inside?
I wish he would come up.

(I came across this poem, which Alan had written, while going through his writings looking for clues as to why he had wanted so badly to die.)

Onset of Illness

Reading Alan's diary after his death I came across the first reference to all not being well with him. An entry for 7 January 1999 reads: 'Not feeling too happy, could be tiredness'; 8 January: 'Feeling better than yesterday'; 9 January: 'Had a good enough day, but there is still something wrong with me'; 11 January: 'Slept for fifteen hours and didn't eat for over twenty-four hours. Still not hungry. There is definitely something up with me'; 14 January: 'Woke up at 3 a.m. and couldn't get back to sleep. Thoughts all over the place'; 15 January: 'Really happy today'; 16 January: 'Feeling down after being so happy yesterday'; 18 January: 'Can't describe how I feel, but my stomach feels queasy, as if I'm going to face something really frightening. Feel really weird'. Subsequent entries show that Alan was experiencing fairly frequent mood swings at this time. He battled on with these feelings and moods and would not see a doctor because most of the time he felt fine. I noticed that these episodes appeared to occur in cycles. Alan would be 'normal' for a while, and he would be entertaining, alive and full of energy. Then his natural good humour seemed to escalate slightly. Immediately following these periods of high good humour there would be periods of depression, when he would sit around, energy depleted, showing no interest in life. At these times he could also be quite prickly and irritable and I would be exasperated with him and my heart would go out to him in equal measure.

After a few days of depression, I would hear the vacuum cleaner going in his room or the guitar being played or his step would quicken around the house, and the 'real' Alan would be back with us. The 'highs' were barely discernible, but the low moods were more noticeable. Even now I suppose some members of our family would argue that Alan did not have a mental illness, however, a mother reading this will probably agree that we can be highly intuitive where our children are concerned and acutely aware of nuances of feeling in them. We seem to see and sense things about them that are not so obvious to others, sometimes even to their own siblings.

I realise that this description of Alan's illness does not read like the black hole that causes some people to take their lives, but any other description would be an exaggeration. Had his illness been more discernible and had he not been so determined to battle with it and disguise it for so long because he saw it as a flaw in his character, Alan might well be with us today. He would have had no choice but to have treatment if his illness had impaired his everyday functioning to a greater extent than it did. I believe that the lucky ones are those who seek help early and are not afraid to see depression as just another eminently treatable illness.

Successful Treatment with Medication
According to the Irish Association of Suicidology, at any given time one in ten young people between the ages of thirteen and nineteen experience a major depression. We can live with depression as we can live with diabetes. In fact, in many cases, just a few months' treatment with medication and/or counselling is all that is needed and the person goes on to live a normal life and is never bothered again by depression. Again, in some cases the depression returns and may need further short-term treatment, and this may be repeated throughout a person's life. In other

cases a person may have ongoing clinical depression, which can be controlled by medication and can allow the person to live a normal life by just taking a tablet every day. An illness that has the potential power to cripple or kill can, in fact, be rendered ineffectual quite easily by accessing medical help at an early stage.

George H. Colt, in his book *November of the Soul,*[1] says that of the nearly three hundred mental illnesses listed, a few are particularly associated with suicide. They are schizophrenia, borderline personality disorder and alcohol and drug abuse. However, the disorder that suicide is most closely associated with is depression. Many people do not realise that depression can cause such a wide range of problems or so much pain. A lot of people who are depressed do not take their condition seriously enough, having the mistaken belief that depression comes from weakness or a character flaw. This myth is what caused Alan to conceal his depression. Because he was embarrassed he avoided getting help. It is well known that untreated depression, as it progresses, can lead to suicidal ideation. I see education about mental illness, especially depression, as it is so prevalent among young people today, as a vital element in the overall education of young people of all ages in secondary schools.

Diagnosis

In November 2001 Alan was diagnosed with 'a mild cyclical disorder and some depression' by a psychiatrist. A low dose of anti-depressant medication was prescribed and it was recommended that he attend group therapy sessions. The latter was anathema to Alan, who would not disclose his feelings even to his closest friends. I know that if group therapy were recommended to me – even now with my experience of group work and having a healthy self-confidence – I would be resistant to it. It makes sense to me that it is not for every person, even though it is seen to be very successful in the treatment of depression. To me, group therapy is something that Alan may have responded to further along the road of treatment than the initial assessment session, however, I was so relieved that Alan had agreed to see a psychiatrist after years of trying to persuade him to get professional help that I did not think too much about anything except the possibility of him finally being free of this illness.

As well as the anti-depressant medication, part of Alan's treatment was a weekly session at a psychiatric clinic, which normally lasted about fifteen minutes. I knew Alan well enough to know that he would be assuring his psychiatrist that he was fine and that all was well. He hated the idea that he was ill and would try to get these sessions over with as quickly as possible. The anti-depressant medication began to take effect after a couple of weeks and Alan's moods seemed to stabilise. He appeared to be less anxious and more at ease. Unfortunately, he began to gain weight, which can be a side-effect of some anti-depressants for some people, and this upset him. Alan was into sport in a big way – the only sports fan of all our children – and a good part of his week consisted of football training, going to the gym and swimming, then playing a football match on a Friday evening. Being physically fit and healthy was of great importance to him, so when he began to gain weight he stopped taking his medication.

Sudden Withdrawal from Medication
When I learned that Alan had stopped his medication, I was worried because I knew that he should have come off it very gradually and only under the supervision of his doctor. Alan thought that because he felt well he could man-

age the mood swings, anxiety and depression himself. I told him of my worry and he assured me that he was fine and would manage. Deep down I felt very uneasy and every day I prayed that he would be relieved of this dreadful illness, which now seemed to be ruling his life. After Alan died I did some research into the medication that he had been taking and learned that three or four weeks after ceasing to take it severe withdrawal symptoms can appear without warning. These can include mood swings, feelings of violence and suicidal ideation. It was three weeks after stopping that Alan took his life. I believe that while Alan's decision to stop taking the medicine may have been a contributory factor to his completing suicide at that particular time, his suicidal thoughts had existed well before he had taken any medication.

The warnings and recommendations that come with prescribed medicines are there to be read. We as lay persons can be intuitive about our body and what is bad or good for it, and can sometimes know more in this area than a medical person, but mental illness by its nature clouds the mind and we can put ourselves in extreme danger by not taking medical advice. Alan was told of the danger he could be putting himself in and made the choice to go ahead with his decision to quit the treatment.

Telling Me of His Plan
Some time before finally ending his life – it could have been days or weeks, I cannot say at this stage – Alan came to me and handed me a blue nylon rope, wrapped in packaging and still unopened, saying, 'Here Mam, take this. I was going to use it, but I won't.' We sat down together and, looking back, all I can see is the inadequacy of my response. I was dying inside. I remember saying to him, 'Alan, I love you so much, please don't do this to me. If you

go I will go with you. I would not be able to live without you.' He replied, 'I won't, Mam, I wouldn't have the courage to do it.' I reminded him that opting out of life was not a courageous act and in my ignorance of the unpredictable and complex nature of depressive illness, I believed that all of us could think rationally no matter what we are going through and that we can get through it. I did not realise then that depression is so insidious, that it can ambush a person and alter rational decision and behaviour if untreated. 'Severe depression can be a life-threatening illness in that one common symptom is a wish to die', says Maggie Helen. She goes on to say, 'Suicidal thoughts can spring into the mind for no apparent reason, and the individual can become immersed in them.'[2]

By handing me the rope, Alan was putting me in the picture, allowing me access to what was going on in his mind; he was reaching out for help. I asked questions, I offered him comfort, I acknowledged his pain, I assured him that I would always be there for him no matter what, I used all the techniques that I knew, as well as my own instinctive response as a mother, and I believed that by talking so openly and giving me the rope, Alan had passed his crisis moment and that this had been a positive turning-point for him. I was only too happy to discuss strategies for moving on. I was actually cheered by the way Alan was able to give me plenty of reasons for living that night. My ignorance of the severity of his condition enabled me to convince myself that all might now be well. I did not take into consideration the sudden dark thoughts and impulses that can come out of the blue and overwhelm the person with depressive illness.

In retrospect, here was my cue to go to see his psychiatrist myself and get advice, but I did not see it. I have no idea why I didn't take this action. Maybe I was so worried and so involved in the situation, or wanted so much to believe that Alan wouldn't kill himself, that I had dug my head ever deeper into the sandpit of denial. I look at myself seven years later and know that I would have moved mountains, no matter what it took, to see my child happy again, so why did I not try to move them that night? When Alan had gone to bed I sat shaking and going back over our conversation, when I should actually have picked up the phone to get professional advice. I have asked myself since why, why, why did I not take action there and then to protect my child from this destructive thing that was tugging at him to destroy himself? I have no answer to this.

Importance of Working in Partnership

From researching suicide I have learned that family members in the situation that I was in that night can feel overwhelmed and so afraid of doing or saying the wrong thing that they can become paralysed. They may feel that if their relationship with the family member at risk and a good family life has not prevented things from getting this bad, then there is nothing they can do. Apparently these reactions are common and understandable, but misinformed. I learned that this thinking can interfere with the many important contributions that caring relatives can make to help, protect and support the suicidal person; that the understanding provided by family members can be a key factor in making professional interventions effective, and the most helpful situations are those where families work in partnership with mental health professionals. The family are the people who know the distressed person best and have been able to observe the person before and since the onset of illness. The family knows the person in an intimate way that the mental health professional does not, because only one aspect of the ill person's story is being presented to them. With family involved, a more comprehensive picture of the person can be drawn.

Forms of Depressive Illness

It may be worthwhile to devote the rest of this chapter to looking at the different forms that depression can take, to explore the signs of depression and to take a look at the causes and effects of depression. I am including this because I have found it very helpful in trying to understand this illness and it may be of value to other families who are trying to come to grips with it.

Reactive Depression: This is where a person responds to a stressful event in life, for example, bereavement, illness, job loss or divorce. Symptoms usually occur very soon after the event, cause distress and can impair everyday functioning. However, with time, the sufferer can move on from the depression and engage in a healthy way with normal life again.

Major or Clinical Depression: At least four or all of the following symptoms should last for most of the day, almost every day, for at least two weeks for a diagnosis of clinical or major depression to be made: depressed mood; a decrease in interest or pleasure in most activities; significant weight loss or gain; fatigue or loss of energy; feelings of worthlessness or excessive guilt; difficulty thinking, concentrating and making decisions; repeated suicidal ideation.

Dysthymic Disorder (dysthymia): A chronic mild depression which manifests as a nearly constant depressed mood for at least two years, accompanied by at least two or more of the following: decrease or increase in appetite; difficulty sleeping or over-sleeping; low energy or fatigue; low self-esteem; difficulty concentrating or making decisions; feeling hopeless. Symptoms usually occur for a couple of months at a time. Generally, this type of depression is described as having persistent but less severe depressive symptoms than clinical or major depression, which could be the reason why people with dysthymia would be less inclined to seek medical help than those with a more pronounced set of symptoms.

Manic Depression (now more often referred to as bipolar disorder): This includes periods of mania and depression. Cycling between these two states can be rapid, or mania alone can be present without any depressive episodes. A manic episode consists of a persistent elevated or irritable mood that is extreme, which lasts for at least one week. At least three of the following features will also be present: inflated feeling of self-importance; decreased need for sleep; more talkative than usual; racing thoughts or ideas; being more easily distracted than usual; increased goal-orientated activity or ideation; over-spending; careless sexual activity; unwise business investments. The symptoms vary from mild, which was the case with Alan, to severe, which often requires hospitalisation and can include psychotic features like hallucinations and/or delusions.

Endogenous Depression: This is defined as feeling depressed for no apparent reason (endogenous means 'from within the body').

There are other types of depression, for example, post-natal, Seasonal Affective Disorder and anxiety depression, however, the five types mentioned above are those that are the most serious and progressive. Although, 80 per cent of people with these conditions respond to counselling and/or antidepressant medication within weeks.[3]

Common Causes

Depressive illness can be caused by hereditary factors, constant setbacks in life, bereavement, illness, relationship break-up, financial difficulties, perceived disconnectedness (a feeling of not belonging), parental divorce, emotional neglect, prolonged absence from a source of care and nurturance, physical and sexual abuse, bullying, food allergy/nutritional deficiency, substance abuse and some medical conditions such as hypothyroidism or hormonal imbalance.

Effects of Depression

The effects of depressive illness are similar in adults and adolescents alike and include drug and alcohol misuse, low self-esteem, feeling ugly or unworthy, the development of eating disorders, self-harming, agitation, aggression, high-risk behaviour, gloominess, suicidal ideation and/or attempted suicide and anti-social behaviour.

Some Myths About Depression

I have come across a lot of myths surrounding the topic of depressive disorders in my research, which I would like to share as I close this chapter. Most have to do with adolescent depression. Again, this might be helpful to families in understanding the stigma that can be attached to mental illness.

Myth: Adolescents do not suffer from real mental illness, they are just naturally moody.
Fact: One in five adolescents have some type of mental health problem in any given year.

Myth: Mental health problems in adolescents are the result of poor parenting.
Fact: Mental illness has little or nothing to do with parenting.

Myth: We are a happy and good-living family; mental illness does not happen to people like us.
Fact: One in four families is affected by a mental health problem.

Myth: Children are too young to get depressed; what would they have to be depressed about?
Fact: Children can be depressed. As stated earlier in this chapter, at any given time, 10 per cent of children between the ages of thirteen and nineteen will experience a major depressive disorder.

Myth: It's not depression; you're just going through a phase.
Fact: Diagnosis should be left to a professional medical practitioner.

Myth: People who abuse drugs are not sick, they're just weak.
Fact: Over 60 per cent of young people with a substance use disorder have a co-occurring mental health problem.

Myth: Troubled youth just need more discipline.
Fact: Almost 20 per cent of youth in correctional facilities have a serious emotional disturbance and most have a diagnosable mental disorder.[4]

Making Progress

I still sometimes go over the events leading up to Alan's death, feeling that if I had done one last thing I might have saved him. However, I find that I am doing this less than I did in the first couple of years after his death, so I can see that I have made progress. I find that I often need to remind myself that most people who die by suicide have a serious depressive illness that is often unrecognised and undiagnosed; that chemicals in Alan's brain became unbalanced and no amount of love or care or trying to build up his self-esteem could have altered his perception that his situation was hopeless.

This is not to say that intervention in a suicide crisis is worthless, as many suicides can be averted by the intervention of family, friends or school staff, who stay with the young person in crisis and are successful in letting him or her know that they are loved and will be missed. I believe that we should not feel that there is nothing we can do once a person has decided to stop living. Suicide, understanding more about it and finding ways to prevent it is everybody's business. This forms the subject of the next two chapters.

Notes

1. Colt, G.H., *November of the Soul: The Enigma of Suicide*, New York: Scribner 2006, p. 41.
2. Helen, M., *Coping with Suicide*, London: Sheldon Press, 2002.
3. Information sourced from the DSM-V.
4. Colt, *ibid.*

Chapter 6

Suicide

'The man who, in a fit of melancholy, kills himself today, would have wished to live had he waited a week.'

Voltaire

After Alan died I felt a need to learn all I could about suicide in order to understand it myself. The knowledge acquired was of great help to me both personally and in my work with young people. I pass it on here in the hope that it may be of use to the reader, and that my own observations will confirm the reader's own or maybe provide food for thought.

Definition

Edwin Shneidman, an American Psychiatrist who devoted his life to the study of suicide, gives a clear description of it in *The Suicidal Mind*, seeing suicide as 'a loss of human potential, a loss of love and intimacy, a loss of creativity and hope; in short, a loss of the preciousness that is life'. Shneidman coined the word 'psychache' to describe 'the hurt, anguish, soreness, aching pain in the psyche, the mind'. He defines suicide as 'a conscious act of self-induced annihilation, best understood as a multi-dimensional malaise in a needful individual who defines an issue for which suicide is perceived as the best solution'.[1]

The World Health Organisation (WHO)[2] reports that every year, nine hundred thousand people worldwide complete suicide and this represents one death every forty seconds. Worldwide, according to the same report, suicide ranks among the three leading causes of death among those aged fifteen to forty-four.

Figures in Ireland

In Ireland, the average number of registered suicides per year is four hundred and twenty. However, according to the Irish Association of Suicidology (IAS), six hundred could be a more realistic figure, as some road deaths, drownings and poisonings are not established suicides and therefore not registered as such.

WHO reports that Ireland has the seventh highest rate of suicide in people aged fifteen to twenty-four in the EU, and the Central Statistics Office (CSO) reported in July 2007 that 50 per cent of the four hundred and nine suicides registered in 2006 were under twenty-five years old and were mostly men. An article in the *Medical News Today*[3] states that research has shown that children as young as six years of age have presented at casualty departments following attempted suicide. The same article reports research as revealing that for every one person who goes to casualty, there are probably as many as ten who do not.

The debate about actual figures can go on and on, and statistics are essential if we are to build up our knowledge base, but to me, and I have no doubt to many others who have lost a family member to suicide, each person that we hear about who has come to this level of distress, who can see no future and who chooses death over life, breaks our hearts. We grieve for someone's hopeless perception of their future, we grieve for the terrible loss that they are to the world and we grieve especially for those who are left behind, bewildered and broken, trying to understand why this has happened.

A report in the *Evening Herald* in August 2007 stated that eight hundred and fourteen calls were made to Childline by suicidal children and teenagers that year. In the same report the CSO recorded the death by suicide of four children, all under fourteen years of age: three boys and a girl.

Risk Factors

What makes a young child attempt to kill him/herself? What is it that puts the idea of self-annihilation into a young person's head? When researching what felt like a mountain of literature on suicide both for a degree and for this book, I found that every person and every organisation involved in the area of prevention, intervention and postvention of suicide cite the same risk factors with little variation: depressive disorders, poor problem-solving skills, hopelessness, poor resilience, previous suicide attempts, substance abuse, being bullied, behaviour problems, childhood neglect, sexual identity issues, having a negative approach to seeking help, lack of social support, relationship difficulties, academic problems and learning difficulties, to name only a few. I believe that while these are certainly some of the risk factors for suicide, the personality of each individual also needs to be taken into account. People differ in their reactions and in their pain and stress thresholds.

Some Reasons for Suicide

In trying to understand the reason that Alan took his life, I learned that no one knows exactly why people kill themselves.

In *November of the Soul,* Colt quotes psychologist Pamela Cantor: 'People complete suicide for many reasons; some people who are depressed will kill themselves, and some who are schizophrenic will kill themselves, and some people who are fine but impulsive will take their own life. We cannot lump them all together.'

Suicide often occurs shortly after a stress event,[4] for example, a disciplinary crisis, a recent disappointment or rejection, like a relationship break-up, exam failure or failure to get a job. Alan had been working in a men's clothing shop, managing the suit department. He was very popular among the staff and the management were sympathetic to his illness. The nature of his depression meant that occasionally Alan would actually be sick and immobilised by anxiety and could not get out of bed in the morning, and this would perhaps happen a couple of days a month. He was a very good salesman and liked people; he was a charmer who could 'sell sand in the Sahara' and was happy doing his work. It was always at the back of Alan's mind that he had not done as well in school as his brothers. Although he had studied sports physiotherapy, which he was passionate about, he had not had the consistent good health and motivation that further study would have required in order to go into practice. He could not see that what he was doing in his job suited his personality; he was interacting with people, always trying to beat his own targets in sales, always in demand to socialise with his colleagues. A short time before Alan's death he resigned from his job. I asked him what had happened because I had heard him raise his voice on the phone, but all he said was, 'It's okay, Mam, I don't work in ___ any more, but I don't want to talk about it.' I knew better than to pursue the matter, because Alan had been withdrawn and irritable for a couple of days.

Last Day of Alan's Life

On Thursday, 28 February, Alan told me he had an appointment with an employment agency, that he was going for a complete change of occupation, maybe administration in the Civil Service. I thought this was one of the oddest things I had ever heard, as Alan and a nine-to-five, repetitious occupation were polar opposites. I said nothing, but when he came back from the interview he looked very down again and said that he had failed the word-processing test, and the interviewer had told him that he would not be suitable for an administrative position. I remember him looking at himself in the mirror and saying, 'Not only am I fat, blind and mental, but now I'm thick as well!' I shot back with, 'And what about "I'm gorgeous, I'm intelligent, I'm generous, I'm kind, I'm a good guitarist and songwriter, I love my godchild, I'm great fun, I'm a brilliant footballer and an excellent artist, I'm loved, I can get around my mother for anything, I'm spoiled rotten by my family"?' (Maybe that is not exactly what I said then, but it was something along those lines, listing off all that was wonderful about him.) We had a bit of banter about this and then he went off to see a close friend, whom he had been avoiding for a few days while he was feeling bad. These were the last words I was to say to him while he was alive.

I was glad Alan went out, because where some people would have used their experience at the employment agency as motivation to acquire IT skills, Alan's tunnel vision could only allow him to focus on the fact that he had failed. I knew Alan well enough to see that he would perceive this as failure as a person; that he would view his unsuitability for a particular occupation as a total rejection of him as a person. I remember the feeling of relief that once more Alan was coming out of a bad patch (not knowing at the time that either entering or coming out of a period of depression is the time that a suicidal person has the energy to kill themselves). I resolved to have another try at getting him to return to professional care as soon as he was feeling well, but I was never to get the opportunity to do that, because a few hours later he was dead. There were several precipitating factors in Alan's final self-destructive act, yet they cannot be neatly packaged as the reason he completed suicide.

Data from Suicide Attempters

I recently came across a newsletter from the Centre for Suicide Prevention in Alberta, Canada,[5] which reviewed research among people who had attempted suicide and highlighted some of the recurring findings from studies of various groups. It is interesting to see from this, which comes from the direct experience of those who are or were suicidal, the many factors – social, personal and psychological – which can be involved in a person's decision to cease living: loneliness; social isolation; emptiness; disconnection or distance from others; feeling a lack of control over life; escape or relief from an unbearable situation or state of mind; despair; depression; hopelessness; desperation; a dislike or disgust with oneself; low self-esteem; not believing that one is worthy of being valued, loved or cared for by others or that one matters. The most frequently endorsed motives for self-harm reported by attempters are not to die, but to escape and to obtain relief from pain, from the 'psychache' that Shneidman describes.

Describing their own reaction to their suicide attempt, a feeling that was prevalent among attempters was shame – shame related to having thoughts of suicide and to having a mental illness. This feeling was also related to feelings of failure and having lost control, for existing or believing one was a burden. Other reactions experienced following suicide attempt included: sadness, depression, disappointment and emptiness; shock at actually having made an attempt; secrecy to avoid stigma and embarrassment; and astonishment that the attempt was not fatal. The study also revealed that some attempters are hindered from seeking psychiatric help because of shame, a fear of being judged, losing the support of loved ones or believing that one is not important enough to receive help.

Attempters who did get help identified the following as some of the things that were beneficial: a change in physical environment; changing one's self-image to a more positive self-perception; connecting or reconnecting with others, with spiritual beliefs or with one's culture; learning and developing more appropriate or effective coping strategies and problem-solving skills; being treated with kindness, respect, acceptance, and without judgement; being seen as a whole person and not just as someone who is suicidal; being affirmed as a worthwhile person, one who is valued and would be missed; proactively seeking help from family, friends or professionals and being included in discussions of assessment and treatment.

Many mental health professionals agree that people who are going through a depressive episode do not have the energy to complete suicide, however, it is when they are coming out of the depression, when energy begins to return that it is a dangerous time for them. It was so with Alan. (An amusing thought has just struck me as I write: Alan would have hated to be seen as a classic textbook case! I can almost hear him protesting: 'Hey, I wasn't just run-of-the-mill, Mam, I was *special!*' If only Alan's real self had been as confident as the self he showed to the outside world.)

Danger Signs

Suicide Awareness Voices of Education (SAVE) lists the following symptoms and danger signs of suicide on their website:[6] ideation (thinking, talking or wishing about suicide); increase or change in substance use or abuse (alcohol and drugs in a vulnerable person can increase the likelihood of impulsive self-harm and remove inhibitions on suicidal behaviour); withdrawal from family, friends, school, work, hobbies; preoccupation with death; suddenly appearing calmer and happier; making arrangements, setting affairs in order; giving things away, such as prized possessions; high risk-taking and self-destructive behaviour; lack of interest in future plans.

Some of the warning signs that a young person may be suicidal, according to the IAS, would be: truancy; poor school performance; anxiety; withdrawn behaviour; sleep disturbance; aggression; impulsiveness; low frustration tolerance; saying life is not worth living; threats of suicide; change in behaviour; and being in copycat situations where a number of their peers have taken their lives.

Myths

As with depressive illness, there are many myths surrounding suicide. The following information was sourced from the Samaritans and the IAS.[7]

Myth: Those who talk about suicide are the least likely to attempt it.
Fact: Those who talk about their suicidal thoughts do attempt suicide. Research shows that about 80 per cent of people who have taken their lives will have told others about it in the weeks prior to their death or will have done things to indicate their deep despair.

Myth: If someone is going to kill themselves there is nothing anyone can do about it.

Fact: It is possible to reduce the risk of suicide if appropriate help and emotional support are offered, and the fact that they are still alive is proof that part of them wants to be alive. Most people who complete suicide don't want to die; they just want the pain to end.

Myth: Talking to people about suicide can put the idea into their head.

Fact: Raising the issue of suicide with those who are severely depressed or distressed can open the door to therapeutic intervention. Also, allowing a person to talk through their worst fears and feelings could provide them with a lifeline that makes all the difference between choosing life and choosing to die. People already have the idea of suicide; it is in the media constantly. If we ask a person, 'Do you have thoughts of suicide?' we are showing that we understand the depth of their pain, that we care and that we take them seriously; that we are willing to listen if they want to share what they are going through. We are giving the suicidal person an opportunity to dislodge pent-up and painful feelings.

Myth: Suicidal people are fully intent on dying.

Fact: Many people are undecided about living or dying. Many callers to the Samaritans do not want to die but they talk of not wanting to go on living.

Myth: If someone has a history of making cries for help they won't do it for real.

Fact: The group of people most at risk of suicide are those who have attempted it in the past year, and those who have attempted suicide are one hundred times more likely than the general population to die by suicide eventually. On average, four out of ten people who die by suicide will have attempted it earlier.

Myth: Only mentally ill/clinically depressed people make serious attempts at suicide.
Fact: People also at risk are those who are suffering from other forms of psychiatric illness and emotional distress. Although the majority of people who complete suicide are judged to have had some sort of psychiatric disorder – whether diagnosed or not – a proportion of people who take their lives do not suffer from any mental illness.

Myth: A good pumping out in A&E will teach those who make silly gestures a lesson they won't forget.
Fact: An attempted suicide should always be taken seriously. Those at risk of suicide may choose a more certain method next time. Many patients have been alienated and an ideal opportunity for therapeutic intervention missed because of the reception they receive in some casualty departments. The response of hospital staff, family and friends to a person who has attempted suicide can greatly influence their recovery (or, if they take it upon themselves to make a judgement about the person or the suicide attempt, can actually do an immense amount of harm, not least to the level of trust in the relationship if the judgement is made by a family member. Unless you are the one who attempted suicide, you have absolutely no idea what was in the person's head at the time, therefore you cannot possibly make a judgement on the person or the situation).

Myth: Once a person is suicidal, they are suicidal forever.
Fact: People who wish to kill themselves may feel this way

for only a limited period of time. Emotional support can help someone come through a suicidal crisis. Talking and listening can make the difference between choosing to live and choosing to end the pain by dying.

Myth: Suicide can be a blessed relief not just for the individual, but for those that surround him or her.
Fact: For those left behind, the loss of a loved one, particularly in such tragic circumstances, is the start of a nightmare, not the end of it. It leaves profound feelings of loss, grief and guilt in its wake. Bereavement by suicide is an extremely heavy cross to bear and those bereaved need special support, as bereavement itself is a risk factor for suicide.

Myth: If someone is going to complete suicide they will not tell anyone about their intentions and will prepare well in advance.
Fact: Many suicides are completed on impulse.

Myth: People attempt suicide to manipulate others.
Fact: We cannot make a judgement on any suicide attempts.

Suicide is Self-Murder
The Oxford English Dictionary tells us that the word 'suicide' comes from the Latin *'sui'*, meaning 'of oneself', and *'caedere'*, meaning 'to kill'. The reason I draw attention to the etymology of the word is that perhaps some young reader who is thinking about suicide, or someone who has attempted suicide already, will take a close look at the words 'kill' and 'oneself'. To kill is to finish something off, to ensure that it will no longer exist, to utterly destroy something. The word 'suicide' has become part of our

everyday language because we hear it so often, and I feel that it may be losing its impact. When David told me the Danish word for suicide, which translates as 'self-murder', it seemed to convey to me a deeper and more horrible reality than the word 'suicide'. To me, self-murder implies self-hatred, self-anger, self-disgust, wanting to annihilate oneself altogether, because one is worthy only of disgust and hatred and is in no way good or deserving of love. This may sound brutal, but is suicide not a brutal act?

I always fear that we will become complacent about suicide and accept it as just another everyday event. This happened during the Troubles in Northern Ireland; I believe that we heard about so many killings, we did become somewhat acclimatised to murder, certainly in the south of Ireland where we were removed from it. Also, we see in the news some of the most horrific injustices carried out in many parts of the world and again we appear to have become impervious to the impact that the suffering of our fellow humans should have on us. There was a time when we would have conducted a nation-wide charity drive in order to help people who are suffering and we would have considered their suffering an outrage. Their suffering is still an outrage, but to what extent are we shocked into action at seeing it?

I remember working with a group of pre-confirmation boys aged eleven to twelve a few years ago, some of whom told me that they were allowed to play computer games that were designed for adults. They mentioned one particular game that involved graphic sexual activity and murder. Voicing my concern about this to a member of staff later, I was told, 'Welcome to the twenty-first century'. I write about this both to illustrate the point that I made above about becoming inured to killing – whether self-killing or murder – and to highlight the importance of being vigilant about what we expose our children to in their formative years. While an adult may be able to separate these games from real life, young children do not have the same level of discernment and can be greatly damaged by them. These young children may grow into adulthood with a distorted sense of the value and importance of life. It is not beyond the realm of possibility that if murder is acceptable as part of the content of video games, it will eventually become acceptable to include suicide.

I know that learning about the various aspects of suicide does not alleviate the pain of loss or bring a loved one back, however, I believe that it may eventually help to reduce the sense of guilt that families can carry. Knowing that I was not responsible for Alan's death, that it was a combination of factors and not my neglect of him, was an immense help to me in the healing process. I hope that it will benefit others who read this in the same way, even if it seems of little help to know these facts initially.

Notes

1. Shneidman, Edwin S., *The Suicidal Mind*, New York: Wiley, 1996.
2. WHO report, September 2008.
3. *Medical News Today*, 6 November 2007.
4. Quoted in *Treating and Preventing Adolescent Mental Health Disorders*, D.L. Evans et al. (eds), Oxford University Press, 2007.
5. SIEC, *Alert*, No. 70, January 2009, www.suicideinfo.ca.
6. www.save.org.
7. For more information contact: Irish Association of Suicidology, 16 New Antrim St, Castlebar, Co. Mayo, and Samaritans, www.samaritans.ie.

Chapter 7

The 'Why' of Suicide

'Oh my lovely young one
When you took your leave last night
You offered me no teardrops, no kisses, no goodbyes
No simple explanation as you walked out the door
Leaving Tír Na nÓg for Tír Na nOíche.'

Christy Moore

In 2006, males accounted for 78 per cent of suicide deaths registered in Ireland. This prompts the question: why is this percentage so high among men? I have frequently stated in this book that the answer to the 'why?' of suicide is often, if not always, elusive. Still, it is a fact of our human nature to question and to go after answers and this is no less true of me. In my searching I came across a lot of information that helped to broaden my understanding, and because of Alan I was especially interested in suicide amongst young men. But I still can't answer the 'why?' of it. Nonetheless, the information, experience and opinion that I share in this chapter might be of some help in grappling with the fraught question of why so many are opting out of life in this way.

Social Change

In Ireland's recent years of economic fluctuation, disintegrating family structures, declining religious affiliation and ever-changing cultural norms, there are many factors complicating a normal adolescent development. On a daily basis young persons may be dealing with issues such as personal growth, role transition, sexual identity, educational expectations – their own and their parents' – divorcing families, alcohol and drug misuse, violence – both personal and in the media – and depression. Dan Neville TD, president of the Irish Association of Suicidology (IAS), has observed that suicide rates, alcohol misuse, transient residencies, abstention from voting and declining religious solidarity are all indications of social fragmentation and all have increased sharply in Ireland since the 1990s. He cites research in the UK as indicating that people living in areas that have high levels of social fragmentation have higher rates of suicide than those living in areas of social deprivation or poverty. It appears that similar research has not been carried out in this country.[1]

Change in Male Role Identity

Men in our society have mostly moved away from the role of sole breadwinner in the family as more women have taken on careers that involve them being out in the world – in some cases earning more than their partners – in the last three decades or so. Prior to that, society viewed men as having a definitive function in being the only partner who worked outside the home. In a marriage partnership it was usual for the husband to work outside, earning money to keep his family, while his wife worked inside the home, housekeeping and looking after the children. These were generally accepted roles for both parties, although modern women must wonder how this could ever have been acceptable to women in those days. This arrangement had been in place for centuries and it must surely have been difficult for men to accept this change in role identity, even though the hard-won freedom and equality that women now have obviously represents a more just social situation than had previously existed. I believe that it will take a couple of generations to bring such a radical social change to a level that will be accepted as the norm by all of society. It appears to me that there are remnants of this gender inequality very much in place still, however, the majority of young males today are moving with the changes, which began forty years ago.

Working with young people in schools for the past eighteen years, I have had the opportunity to observe this role change closely. I have seen young girls whose grandmothers lived through the time that women began to gain equality in this country, and, two generations later, that precious 'assertiveness', which my generation discovered, is being displayed as 'aggressiveness' by some young girls. The anger that was a major driving force in the liberation of women from oppressive social structures still exists in some of today's young females. This anger may have been passed on to them not only through stories about the oppressive social attitudes that prevailed towards women two generations earlier, but they may also have picked up nuanced attitudes of older significant females. Unfortunately, their rage is directed mostly at the males with whom they interact, and this could compound the confusion that already exists for young men around role identity.

Similarly, some young men may still retain the traditional male 'head of the house' attitude, because it has been so difficult for their fathers and grandfathers to adapt to a social change that would appear to diminish their role in society, and in doing so, could damage their whole sense of identity. I believe that we can put the rage that we see in some young males down to role confusion and lack of a positive social identity, which translates into a lack of a sense of personal identity in many cases. We cannot generalise about these issues, however, because each individual will journey in his or her individual way and at his or her individual pace.

I do not mean to imply that all young females of the present generation carry unconscious rage against oppression by a previously male-dominated society and demonstrate this in aggressive behaviour towards males, however, it is certainly evident and observable behaviour. I have witnessed this behaviour and this attitude many times in the course of my work, and have been affirmed in my observations by young people themselves when I have raised the issue in groups.

Peer Pressure

I have also seen at first hand the expectation to 'be a man' that young males put on each other. One fifteen-year-old boy with whom I have worked, who goes to dance classes, is passionate about dance and is a gifted dancer, was very quick to assure me that he is not 'gay' when asked to demonstrate his talent. I have noticed in groups of young males that they watch each other intently for signs that they are approved of by their peers, and one of the ways that they try to gain approval is by putting on the façade of the 'hard man'. In some groups of young males with whom I have worked, any show of emotion or sensitivity by an individual has provoked either derision or hostility from most of the other members of the group. I am amazed by the large number of young males I have encountered who have a 'black and white' attitude to their masculinity: either you are a 'male' – in which case you display the accepted characteristics of the male, i.e. ability to fight, to conceal any emotion and vulnerability, avoid any intimate self-disclosure and so on – or you are 'gay' or 'girly'. This label can destroy your credibility as a 'man' among the male peer group.

In a school retreat situation, when all is quiet and we are away from the school environment, I address with young males regarding the issues mentioned above and encourage them to be themselves for the day, to drop the 'hard man' act while in this safe space together. They know and I know that we are walking in dangerous waters at these times, because in choosing to remove the façade they are leaving themselves vulnerable to being bullied by one another. They find it so difficult to trust one another, and no one can blame them for that, what with bullying being so prevalent during the teenage years.

On one occasion with a group of boys, I asked them to lie on the floor for meditation. Soft music was playing and I was guiding their imagination when my eye was caught by a big sixteen-year-old rugby player lying curled up on the floor like a little child. I felt tears come to my eyes and spill over because all I saw as I looked at him was the vulnerable little boy that he was not allowed to be in everyday life, but who was present underneath the façade that he had to live behind in order to survive in a male environment. This happened perhaps fifteen years ago, but I can still feel the compassion that washed over me as I looked at him. There are such things as 'graced' moments, when we are given a special insight, and I truly believe that at that moment I was given a glimpse of the emotional struggle of the male adolescent.

I believe that there is a great need to put in place a life-skills programme involving problem-solving and communication skills that would equip young people – especially young men – to talk about emotional issues, so that if they feel that they want to stop living they can go to their families, GPs, teachers or friends and accept the support that will be offered at these critical times.

Substance Abuse

We know from widespread research that alcohol and drug misuse are believed to contribute to depression and other health problems, and can also lead to impaired judgement and heightened impulsiveness. We will look for a moment at alcohol and cannabis abuse – cannabis being the drug most widely used by adolescents and young adults.

We see from autopsy findings reported in the media that alcohol abuse plays a significant role in suicide and features prominently in youth suicide. A study carried out in counties Meath, Louth and Cavan showed that 93 per cent of men under thirty years old had alcohol in their systems when they completed suicide. Colt observes that while there is agreement that suicide and alcohol are closely related, there is less agreement on how they interact: 'Certainly alcohol and depression may form a vicious cycle: drinking can lead to depression and depressed persons often self-medicate by drinking, which may only exacerbate their depression and may, over time, alter the delicate chemistry of the brain.'[2]

Alcohol may be used to escape pain, and when it fails to put enough distance between a person and their pain the ultimate escape of suicide can be chosen: 'Alcohol is a powerful accelerant to suicide rates in Ireland with its combined dis-inhibitory and dysphoric effects, particularly on the young adult brain.'[3] Alcohol itself does not cause people to have suicidal thoughts, but if a person is thinking of suicide, drinking alcohol will reduce inhibition for carrying out the act.

In the years of the 'Celtic Tiger', prosperity in this country yielded greater disposable income, leading to greater spending by young people on alcohol. 'Binge drinking' is a reality in modern youth culture and sessions usually take place out of doors or when parents are away and the house is empty. Drinking parties are held and, along with alcohol, cannabis use at these parties is not uncommon, or so I am informed by some of the young persons who attend them. These activities begin in early adolescence, paving the way for possible mental and social disorder in later years. Peer pressure to take part in these activities is high and the young adolescent can be faced with exclusion from the group or with ridicule for being 'chicken', as well as other forms of bullying if he or she does not join in. Fear of rejection is a potent emotion in any of us, but in adolescence it can take on titanic proportions.

In the course of a year I would conduct a retreat with approximately five thousand students, and over the years I have observed the age when young people begin to smoke, drink alcohol and engage in sexual activity becoming lower and lower.

The drinking habits of adolescents are not the only contributory factor to problems with alcohol. It is well documented that excessive drinking by parents can have a detrimental effect on the well-being of a child. I have listened to many adolescents throughout the years tell me that they dread going home because their mother might be drunk, or that they are afraid to go home because they may be beaten by either parent who could be drunk. Some young people do not have the opportunity to do homework or to study because they need to look after younger siblings or a drunken parent. Some of these are too ashamed to speak out in school about their family situation and, therefore, can be regarded by their teachers as lazy and uncaring. They suffer punishment rather than show what they see as disloyalty to their parents by telling the truth of their situation.

Research shows that destructive family patterns and traumatic events in childhood affect young people's lives thereafter, especially when they have been unable to cope with the trauma. The World Health Organisation cites the following aspects of family dysfunction and instability among the negative life events of suicidal children and adolescents: poor care provided by parents/guardians, poor communication within the family, alcohol and substance abuse or anti-social behaviour in the family. Every single one of our children needs to know that he or she is loved, valued and respected; they are the life and soul of the next generation.

Cannabis is Not a Harmless Substance
Findings from a Dutch survey reported in the *British Journal of Psychiatry* show that cannabis use in adolescence increases the likelihood of experiencing symptoms of schizophrenia in adulthood. An adolescent using cannabis has a six times greater chance of developing a psychosis by the age of twenty-six than a non-user. According to the report, several studies show associations between cannabis use and depressive disorders when tobacco and alcohol use were added to the mix. Association between cannabis use and attention problems was significant and, therefore, the use of cannabis could be associated with poor school performance. It was also found in this study that cannabis use is associated with aggression and delinquency.[4]

Sexual Identity
Issues involved in understanding sexual identity can be difficult for adolescents and young adults. As they come to

terms with their sexuality they may experience isolation, depression and bullying, which can lead to a higher risk of suicide ideation. It has been observed that the history of homosexuality is strikingly similar to the history of suicide, as over the millennia both were viewed as a natural act, then as a sin and a crime, then as a disease. Just as the bodies of suicides were dragged through the streets, hung upside down and burned, homosexuals were imprisoned, beaten, castrated, burned at the stake and hanged in public squares. 'For centuries', writes Colt, 'exposure in a homophobic society, and the attendant public humiliation, possible imprisonment and loss of friends, family and career, almost literally meant the end of one's life. Many homosexuals saw no option but to make that figurative end literal.'[5]

In 2007, Finian McGrath TD called for research into the role of homosexuality in the suicides of young men. McGrath claimed that recent research in the US indicates that one-third of American teenage suicide victims were young homosexual males. McGrath said that his own work within the homosexual community would appear to back up this statistic. He noted that almost all homosexual males with whom he works have said that the worst period in their lives occurred during adolescence when they were coming to terms with the fact that they had a homosexual orientation. McGrath stated in the report that 'for many it was a nightmare, a very traumatic time as they struggled with the competing desire to come out and tell family and friends'. He went on to say that their fear of rejection and bullying was immense, should their status become known in the wider community.[6]

Colt observes that 'stigma, internalised homophobia and the spectre of AIDS are factors that may be especially daunting for homosexual adolescents, for whom suicide seems to be a particular danger'. He goes on to say that numerous studies show higher rates of depression, panic disorder and anxiety among homosexual members of society than among those who are heterosexual. Colt sees this as a result of having to live on the margins of society. Among homosexual people, rates of alcohol and drug abuse – risk factors for suicide in any group – are estimated to be three times higher than in the general population, according to Colt, and he does not find this surprising 'given that for many years gay and lesbian socialising revolved around bars, one of the few places where they were able to gather comfortably'. Alcohol and drugs are also ways in which someone might deal with social stigma.[7]

According to President Mary McAleese: '[A]lthough Ireland is making considerable progress in developing a culture of genuine equality and recognition and acceptance of gay men and women, there is still an undercurrent of both bias and hostility which young gay people must find deeply hurtful and inhibiting. For them, homosexuality is a discovery, not a decision, and for many it is a discovery which is made against a backdrop where, within their immediate circle of family and friends as well as the wider society, they have long encountered anti-gay attitudes which will do little to help them to deal openly and healthily with their own sexuality.'[8]

Bullying

The issue of bullying arises in almost every retreat that I lead with a group of adolescents. It seems to me that bullying is something that is extremely difficult to eradicate, because a lot of the time we have a fuzzy definition of what bullying is. 'But I was only messing', is a protest that I hear very often from young people who are genuinely not aware that they are doing harm. Some examples of bullying are:

- spreading rumours;
- insulting someone by word or behaviour, particularly on the grounds of race, age, gender, disability, sexual orientation or religious belief;
- exclusion or victimisation;
- ridiculing or demeaning another person;
- making threats or negative comments;
- deliberately undermining another person by constant criticism;
- 'slagging' someone.

The whole area of bullying is vast and much research is ongoing, however, for the purpose of this book I will confine the discussion to that of bullying among adolescents. Bullying is not always face-to-face. It can occur in written communications, email or by phone, and I have met children as young as eleven in sixth class who have received text messages on their phone saying insulting things like 'you're ugly', 'you're fat', 'I hate you and everybody hates you'. This must produce feelings of anger, humiliation and anxiety in a young person, and the resultant stress can lead to loss of self-confidence, unhappiness and fear.

Norwegian researcher Dan Olweus defines bullying as 'when a person is exposed, repeatedly and over time, to negative actions on the part of one or more persons'. He defines negative action as when 'a person intentionally inflicts injury or discomfort upon another person, through physical contact, through words or in other ways'. Olweus also points out that bullying has been found to have long-term effects, including depressive symptoms and poor self-esteem in adulthood; that many adults who have been victimised as children in school often have clear and vivid memories of these events.[9]

The effects of bullying can be very serious and even fatal: 'Bullying changes lives. It can drive people to the edge of despair and beyond. The anxiety experienced by a young person who is bullied can make it impossible for him or her to learn effectively, and this can cause long-term damage to self-esteem and achievement.'[10] One of the most critical factors precipitating suicidal ideation arising from interpersonal problems is humiliation. Feelings of disgrace and public disparagement may shatter a young person's healthy narcissism and sense of identity, and that a loss of a basic sense of one's worthiness is a powerful force to increase thoughts of self-annihilation.

Research results show that the pain of rejection and isolation is much greater than the occasional kick or punch. An Irish study of suicidal ideation in adolescents found that almost half of the sample gave school factors including bullying as the main reason why someone might want to kill themselves and, according to Dr Mona O'Moore of the Anti-Bullying Centre, Trinity College: 'There is a growing body of research which indicates that individuals, whether child or adult, who are persistently subjected to abusive behaviour are at risk of stress-related illness which can sometimes lead to suicide.'[11]

Childhood Abuse
There are many ways that a child can be maltreated or abused. It might be deliberate physical injury or neglect, emotional bullying or intimidation, prolonged social isolation and the withdrawal of affection or the exploitation of a child through sexual abuse. The horrific effects of such abuse and neglect on a child's self-esteem and behaviour has been well documented in recent times. Children who

have been victimised in this way live with a sense of power-lessness, guilt and inadequacy that is crippling.

Research has demonstrated a strong connection between childhood abuse and later suicidal behaviours, with the link being strongest when the abuse has been of long duration, when the perpetrator has been known to the victim and when the abuse involves force. Those with a history of childhood maltreatment have been shown to be three times more likely to become depressed or suicidal compared with those who have not been abused, with the risk of repeated suicide attempts an alarming eight times greater for youth with a sexual abuse history.[12]

Throughout my own secondary school days I personal-ly felt that I was dying inside, having suffered sexual abuse by a family friend just before I started secondary school. I kept the abuse to myself out of fear and confusion and a desire to protect my parents from the pain of knowing that this had happened to me. However, inside I wanted to be heard and that is one reason why I have devoted the last eighteen years of my life to listening to young people who are perhaps experiencing some of the same feelings that I did; young people for whom every day is a struggle to be heard and to feel that they matter to the world. Arising out of my own experience I have a close affinity and empathy with adolescents. The reason I raise this issue here is that soon after Alan's death I was told that he had been sexual-ly abused by a trusted neighbour. This went a long way for me in explaining Alan's anger and low self-regard, and I believe that this compounded his depression. I do not deny the existence of a chemical imbalance in him, but I will always wonder – because his illness was so mild – that had he not suffered this ordeal, would he still be with us? We will never know and I still find it very difficult to live with my own guilt that I was not there to protect him.

I grew up in a loving family who had no idea of the extent of my own inner suffering, just as I was not fully aware of all the reasons behind Alan's pain. Over the years I have heard so many young people tell me the same thing: that their family members have no idea of the pain that they carry within themselves. I have also heard of the difficult circumstances in which some young people have to live: some young person may dread going home because of parental conflict; others may be caught up in the separation or divorce of parents and may have torn loyalties; still others are struggling to meet their own or their parents' academic expectations. I have listened to the stories of young people coping with life in extremely difficult circumstances, who plough on and do not consider 'opting out'. Then again I have listened to the young person for whom there is no apparent reason to be suicidal, yet who are experiencing profound inner pain and for whom the idea of suicide holds the only hope of relief.

This chapter has only touched on some of the negative life situations that could lead a young man to take his life. Admittedly, a lot of the content of this discussion can also be applied to young females, and indeed the suicide rate among females is rising all the time. I have focussed mainly on males because of my experience with Alan's suicide and because I am not sufficiently familiar with the research findings on female suicide to comment.

Having said this, it must also be acknowledged here that the negative life events and situations mentioned in this chapter do not always or inevitably lead to suicide. As we know, suicide and its causes cannot be neatly packaged; we are still searching for the reason, or the combination of reasons, that pushes a person over the edge of the precipice.

Notes

1. Dan Neville TD, Chairman of IAS.
2. Colt, *ibid.*, p. 272.
3. Hayes, M., Chairman of the Advisory Committee for the Ireland Funds, *Mental Health: Healing the Hurt*: www.irl-funds.org/ireland/news.
4. Sudak, H.S., Ford, A.B. and Rushworth, N.B., 'Adolescent Suicide: An Overview' in *American Journal of Psychotherapy*, Vol. 38, 1984, pp. 350–363; British Journal of Psychiatry, Vol. 188, 2006, p. 148–153.
5. Colt, *ibid.*, p. 261.
6. Reported in *Sunday Independent*, 7 October 2007.
7. Colt, *ibid.*, p. 264.
8. President McAleese addressing delegates at the World Conference of the International Association for Suicide Prevention in Killarney, 2007.
9. Olweus, D., *Bullying in Schools: What We Know and What We Can Do*, Oxford: Blackwell, 1993, p. 48.
10. Pffefer, C., *Suicide in Children and Adolescents*, Toronto: Hogrefe & Huber, 1990, pp. 65–88.
11. Anti-Bullying Centre, Trinity College, Dublin.
12. *Canadian Incidence Study of Reported Child Abuse and Neglect*, Ottawa: Health Canada, 2001: www.hc-sc.gc.ca.

Chapter 8

Suicide is a Spiritual Issue

'God created the man in the image of himself,
In the image of God he created him;
Male and female, he created them.
God saw all that he had made, and indeed it was
very good.'

(Genesis 1:27, 31, The Jerusalem Bible)

In previous chapters I have referred to the sense of inadequacy and worthlessness that Alan experienced with varying degrees of intensity throughout his life. These feelings are a common experience that many will relate to. Most people will move on from these feelings or at least become able to balance them with an awareness of their own goodness and value. Often in my work I will invite young people to list their own good points – extreme reluctance is the inevitable response, even when the list is to be written and seen by no one but themselves. If asked to speak about their negative points, the room becomes alive with group members only too willing to share openly all the things they would like to change or dislike about themselves.

While in some ways these reactions may be predictable in a group situation, they do underline the reality that many of us are quick to condemn ourselves and that this default position becomes ingrained in us at a very young age. In this chapter, I want to explore how this lack of self-belief and dearth of self-love runs totally contrary to a healthy spirituality and to a connection with the God in whose image we are made. To me, it is a dis-ease of the spirit, which often goes unrecognised. To believe we are nothing of worth is incompatible with belief in the God who created us and saw that 'it was good'. As I was to discover, Alan had reached a similar conclusion, one which I would dearly love to have been able to challenge and help him to reconsider.

A Sense of Connectedness

After Alan's death I found a sheet of paper in his room on which he had written, 'I don't believe in God and I don't believe in myself!' It struck me that Alan was saying, 'I don't believe in God *therefore* I don't believe in myself.' This to me was a cry from a soul in anguish; from someone who had known at a profound level that to have trust in God would have strengthened him to believe that he was a person of immense value and importance to the world. It is my belief that to have a deep awareness of this value and connectedness to God may have given Alan a reason to live, a reason to hope, a reason to look within himself and to see that his life had meaning and purpose.

Alan also wrote, 'How can I truly love anybody if I don't love myself?' Had he had a sense of this intimate connect-edness of his spirit to the Spirit of God within, it could have brought about a respect for himself and a desire to love himself and others with a compassionate love. It seems that as we grow in love and compassion for our-selves, our love and compassion for others becomes deep-er and more sincere. Somehow knowing and believing at a deep level that within us lies perfect love, perfect justice, perfect truth and perfect beauty – all traits of God – can animate us, give us life, urge us to believe in ourselves and reach out to others. The knowledge that 'made in the image of God' means just what it says – that we actually are part of the Spirit of God, which is constantly at work within us transforming our human, imperfect selves – can be a galvanising force to strengthen us at the worst of times.

Going Within to Find the True Self

Like a lot of other people who have taken their lives, Alan came to a point where he could not see beyond what was immediately visible. Yet by writing what he did, I believe that although he could not see or feel, he could sense that there was Something or Someone to whom he was intimately connected. If only he could have turned to that Other – which I call God – he would have known that he was not on his own, but was connected to the Creator of all that is and to every other living thing in the world. We can look to others to try to find an authentic self-worth, as so many of us do, but I have learned that real self-esteem comes from within, from knowing how valuable I am to God, to myself and to others in my world. I need to be self-aware in order to find my true worth and I have discovered that only by making time in my busy life for solitude, stillness and reflection can I come to know who I truly am, know that I am part of all created things and part of the Creator. This knowledge of who I am, of how my existence has meaning and purpose in the world, generates a real desire to go beyond my own ego towards an authentic respect for myself and to reach out to others in sincere love and compassion.

A very simple exercise I use with young people to illustrate the importance of nurturing our spiritual selves is as follows: I draw a circle representing a person, calling it a 'pizza'. I then divide the circle into five sections, cutting the 'pizza' into five slices: a social slice, a physical slice, a spiritual slice, an intellectual slice and an emotional slice. I will remove one slice, for example, a social slice, and we can see from this that we do not have a whole 'pizza' any more, that we need interaction with others. If I remove the emotional slice, we will not be able to have feelings. If I remove the intellectual slice, we will not be able to learn, and so on. I go through all the slices, each time showing that we cannot have a full 'pizza' if one slice is missing. I have used this exercise for years in order to demonstrate the importance of paying equal attention to our spiritual, emotional, physical, mental and social selves, and to me it is an important way to begin a retreat with young people in which we will be focussing on ways to nurture our spirit.

For some of us, a way of attending to our spirit could be reading an inspirational book, attending religious services and meetings, listening to music, taking a walk in the countryside and focussing on the beauty around us, contemplating the sky or the sea or the intricate design of a flower or a leaf, or appreciating great art, architecture or poetry. It could be joining a voluntary organisation and helping people in need. It could also mean just making time every day to be still, emptying our mind of worries and distractions, and being in the present moment. Anything that inspires in us a sense of our connectedness to creation and our Creator nourishes our spirit, and each of us will find our own way of coming to know our connectedness.

I find that taking time alone every day to just be in the present moment, simply being aware of the presence of God within me, not thinking about how or why God is within me but just sitting with this reality, provides this feeling of connectedness to the vastness of God and the world.

Blind Trust

I am not saying that because I believe I am part of God and God is part of me that I am immune to suicidal impulses or mental or psychological anguish. Spirituality is situated in the here and now, in the joys and sorrows of everyday life. In the first weeks and months following Alan's death I certainly did not feel that I was of any use to myself or anybody else, spiritually or otherwise. I had no *feeling* of connectedness, but knowing from past experience that I am intimately connected to God within assured me that even in this darkness I had something to hold on to, indifferent as God appeared to be at that time. It is my experience that the more I go through painful times with nothing to hold on to but blind trust, the greater God's Spirit grows in me and, consequently, the deeper my hope and trust grow.

It is crucial to reiterate here that when going through dark times it is impossible to *feel* hopeful and devastated simultaneously, and to *feel* that things will get better. At these times, for me, there is a barely discernible – certainly not accessible – spark of hope somewhere deep within. This spark of hope is generated by blind trust that this God, who appears to have gone missing from life, will return. A friend once said to me: 'Remember in the darkness what you experienced in the light.' This has stayed with me and has helped me enormously in my journey through life. I have had reason to remember it many times, although after Alan's death I could not think of darkness or light or anything other than trying to muddle through the first weeks and months of anguish, just wishing that I had my child with me again.

A Sense of Hope

Today my spirituality gives me hope – an expectation of contentment, of fulfilment, of joy – but it does not tell me to hope for these things at some future time at the expense of enjoying them now. My hope, my expectation, is that I will always know that these are within me and are not dependent on negative or positive circumstances in my exterior life or on the approval of others. That is not to say that I will never again be devastated by loss or angered by injustice; it is not to say that I will never have moments when I am so depressed by situations in my life that I am near to despair. However, it *is* to say that when I reflect on these negative situations, my hope allows me to struggle to see beyond the immediate difficulty, to notice ways in which I can learn and grow from it and to recognise that it will pass and that joy will resurface eventually. It has taken years to come to this point in my life. Surviving the loss of Alan has brought out a new strength in me and given me a renewed awareness of other's, and my own, importance to a God who loves us. This allows me to know in my heart that there is always a worthwhile life beyond the pain. It also lets me know that not only do I belong to God, but that I belong right here, right now, where I am in my life, and that no matter what happens, it *will* be okay.

A Sense of Gratitude

My sense of belonging engenders in me a profound sense of gratitude that I have survived the worst that could happen to me. Some might say that I have an unrealistically optimistic or 'Pollyanna' spirituality, but quite honestly I am hopeful and optimistic because it is my basic nature to be that way, and I have had a sense of intimacy with God for many years, well before Alan's death. This sense of intimacy causes me to feel that I am a good and worthwhile person, with a purpose for being in the world. I emphasise it here to provide an example of how a sense of connectedness to God directly impacts on a positive sense of self.

Spirituality is Individual and Grounded in Everyday Life
Above I have consciously written in the first person because spirituality – our way of being in the world – is as unique to us as our fingerprint. The way that I experience God in my life and in the world may not be the same as whoever is reading this. I know that losing a child to suicide can turn some people away from having anything to do with God, and I have known many people who became totally disillusioned with a supposedly loving Being who could inflict such sadness. A parent can cry out, 'Why did you let my child die?' and then feel guilty for being angry with God. This anger is totally understandable, but I believe that when we cry out honestly to God, whether in anger, pain, joy or any other emotion, it is still prayer and it is still heard and understood.

Spirituality is not other-worldly, but grounded in honesty, in the mud and the fog, the injustices, insecurities, joy and sadness that are part of daily living. It is a hard slog and it involves letting go of feeling judged, unaccepted, unapproved of by God, as well as letting go of being 'nice' to God as we were told to be 'nice' to a visiting great-aunt! I don't think that we can just accept being loved unconditionally by reading about it or by hearing about it. I believe that a healthy spirituality involves trying to understand what unconditional love is, in a world where we may have been brought up to believe that love is conditional on our behaviour: 'I will love you if you're good, happy, don't upset me, pass your exams or are good-looking.' The difficulty lies in letting go of all this and learning that God is Love itself and is incapable of not loving! We are all beloved human beings whether we choose to acknowledge God or not. It is my experience that when we finally come to a true realisation of the depth of God's love for us, we cannot but begin to love ourselves and see ourselves as persons of great worth and value. To me, the greatest gift I ever received was learning that I could be my flawed, human self in God's presence and still be loved utterly.

Reaching Out

Accepting that we are loved in this way can help us to move slowly forward. In my case, I experienced a renewed sense of purpose, which made me want to share my experience and what I have learned from it with others. I realise now that as soon as I sensed the tiny voice inside, felt the first stirring of wanting to reach out to troubled young people, I was even more convinced of what I had known for most of my life – that I am part of God and God is part of me. I also realised that I was not on my own to cope with my pain; that it could be transformed into something that could help others. This certainly was not a desire that came from me; I was far too preoccupied with trying to survive the pain of each day to think of anyone outside of my family. No, my part was to recognise the stirring in my spirit and to just say, 'Yes'. This is an awesome thought: that this vast and perfect Other to whom I am intimately connected, and who knows the real me with all my faults and failings, would give me the desire and provide the resources necessary for me to go out and make a difference in the world, and not because of anything I had done to deserve it.

All the same, as I was going about this, I struggled with the grief that I thought would never subside. Somehow I was given the courage to stand up in front of groups of students, tell my story and answer their questions calmly and honestly. This took a lot of emotional energy and I was shattered *after* these talks, but always peaceful *during* them. This phenomenon is further proof to me of the existence of God within me and within all of us – a God who is always on our side, who suffers with us and who gives us the strength and love that we need in the worst of times.

It is important to attend to our spirit as much as we attend to our body and mind, and a healthy self-worth can be served by a healthy spirituality. For me, hope played a part in moving from crippling grief to once again leading a productive and happy life. These things make it possible to begin moving on, something I will now explore in greater depth.

Chapter 9

Moving On

'Only people who are capable of loving strongly can also suffer great sorrow, but this necessity of loving serves to counteract their grief, and heals them.'

Leo Tolstoy

Giving Time to the Healing Process

From experience, I have learned that the journey to healing is a long and slow process, and can only be undertaken at the bereaved person's own pace, and for all of us this will be different. We need to be aware that even close friends may unconsciously try to pressurise us into hurrying a process that cannot be hurried, if it is to have a successful outcome. Naturally, friends and family want us to feel better, but it is impossible to put a time on this.

Pretending to have 'pulled out of it' or to be 'handling it well' may keep our family or friends happy, but it is ultimately damaging to us. We need unconditional support at this point, not advice, unless our advisor has been there before us, and even then advice should be well considered before being dispensed. Our healing process can involve going backwards sometimes. Anniversaries, birthdays, Christmas and other times can bring fresh waves of grief, but I have found that this lessens as time goes by.

One of the initial signs of being on the road to healing for me was noticing that I was able to begin to make plans for the future. Another was when I accepted that I would never know the whole reason why Alan took his life. From my perspective, accepting Alan's death meant facing up to the reality that my life would have to go on without him, and that it was up to me to decide whether to be permanently hurt or to move on and try to construct a new life. I chose to move on, and even this choice itself took time and pain to make. To achieve moving to where I am now took a long time, and, as I said before, the process cannot be rushed. This new life that I now live contains all my memories of Alan, and a wonderful thing that I have noticed is that I now tend to focus on the happy memories as well as those surrounding his death. There are still times – and I suppose there will always be – when I yearn for him to be back with me; sometimes he is, but only in a dream. When I dream that Alan has come back to me I can feel a happiness, a wholeness, a completeness that I know I can never again feel in my waking life.

Guilt at Moving On

Some of us can feel guilty because we believe that accepting a loved one's death can mean that we don't love them or that we are forgetting about them. Sometimes we can experience feelings of guilt because something has made us laugh or because we have thoroughly enjoyed something. In some way we can feel that we are betraying our loved one by being capable of happiness again.

In the September following Alan's death, we went to Malta for a holiday. One afternoon, while walking on a lovely, peaceful road in the sunshine, I happened to glance into an old garden to see a woman in a flowing summer dress and big straw hat, sitting at an easel, painting. This was an incredibly beautiful scene, like a picture on an old postcard, and I felt as if I had been transported back to a past time when life was more gentle and less cruel. Even in my delight, I experienced a twinge of guilt that I could actually feel so happy and peaceful. It felt as if I was betraying Alan in some way, that if he knew I was feeling happy he might think that I had not loved him enough. I have learned since that this is quite a common feeling among people who are bereaved.

Bereavement Counselling

At a time of bereavement, some people may feel the need to talk about and explore their relationship with a loved one, but are reluctant to burden family or friends with this. Bereavement counselling offers a safe space in which to address issues, whether emotional or spiritual, with someone who has been trained to listen. Five years after Alan died, I realised that I still carried issues surrounding that time, which I had not properly addressed and dealt with. I decided to seek bereavement counselling and here I was able to be completely open without upsetting family or friends; I was free to explore any unfinished business and move beyond bereavement to the new life that I live now. Had I known how beneficial it would be to me, I would have made a greater effort to seek therapy at a much earlier stage. I paraphrase here Henry Thoreau's comment that the greatest compliment that was ever paid me was when one asked what I felt, and attended to my answer.

Today there is a big 'hole' in the family, felt most keenly at gatherings, when we are all together, or at Christmas, which Alan loved. All the same, I am blessed that I can still remember the texture of the skin on his hands and the feel of his back under his shirt when I hugged him. I can almost see him standing at the cooker mashing potatoes to creamy perfection, claiming that he was the only one who could do this properly! I can recall the wonderful times that our house was filled with fun and music, and I can smile at these memories at last, which to me is another indication of acceptance and progress.

Reflections

I asked my family if they would like to contribute a concluding reflection, and Noel and Noelle declined. Noelle is in the process of moving into an apartment – the last of our children to leave the nest – and Noel is still reluctant to revisit his pain publicly. Íde, Alan's girlfriend, who has remained close to our family, agreed to contribute something, along with David, Stephen and Niall.

Niall

I remember in the weeks following Alan's death that I struggled to make some sort of sense of what had happened. The terrible waste of life, of opportunity for living and experiencing. My birthday was at the end of March. I am lucky with my friends and, ironically, it was one of my most memorable birthdays ever. Everyone bought me a present, which can be unusual between male friends. One of the gifts I received was a Ryan Adams album and, as I listened to it the next day, I realised that Alan would have absolutely loved it; it was just his thing. As I thought about this, a wave of sorrow hit me. The gravity of what he had done suddenly became as real again as seeing his body in the ambulance. Not being able to share things that would have given him such delight was heartbreaking.

My dreams in the months following his death were also devastating. He would arrive in the dream, looking fresh and well rested, and we would chat. I would ask him why he killed himself but he didn't want to talk about it. The pattern was mostly the same: there would be two Alans; one would die in the dream and I would experience the pain of his death over again, but then the other would appear and tell me that he was here to stay and wasn't going anywhere. I would be lulled into a warm assurance that he was still in my life and was safe, then I would wake up and after a few moments' disorientation would realise that he had not really come back. I still have this dream from time to time. However, the pain upon waking has lessened.

When Alan left my life so suddenly and in such a violent way I developed a kind of paranoia. In the period following his death I stopped trusting that everything would work itself out. This is certainly not the way I feel about life now, but when something so unexpected and tragic happens on a day like any other, it is almost as if one expects some other catastrophe to occur. As a result, one can erect borders, keeping others at arm's length, and one can trust fewer people. This was my experience and it has taken a lot of work to reverse. Closing my heart and hiding from my emotions did me no good whatsoever, and only through accepting that the feelings were there and needed a voice and needed, above all, to be felt and experienced, did I make serious progress towards healing.

Now the pain of losing Alan is more like an old injury than a raw wound. Time does make a difference. One day you realise that your life is marching on, regardless of whether you are fully aware of your actions and what is happening around you. While there were feelings of unending emotional pain for a long time after Alan died, they are simply not there any more. I am now fully aware of the world around me: its infinite beauty, depth and potential.

Forgiveness and compassion have played a great part in my recovery. Alan was sexually abused as a child and the abuser is known to the police and to our family, but was never brought up on any charge as the case would have been based on hearsay, the evidence having died with Alan. I have forgiven this man for what he did and bear him no ill will. I hope that in his own life he has experienced enough love and healing not to do what he did to anyone else. Through the extremely useful Buddhist practice of Tonglen I have been able to turn what was very potent anger into compassion for any person involved in Alan's death, so that it in no way negatively affects my life now. Compassion and forgiveness for myself has been of paramount importance. I was the last person to speak to Alan alive, and if I had gone to bed twenty minutes later maybe something I said or did would have made a difference. However, I honestly think that if I had stayed up for an extra twenty minutes, he would have just waited and done it anyway. He was determined to end his pain that night.

I loved Alan dearly, he was a brother and a friend and we had our disagreements over the years, but nothing too serious. Being honest, I'm sure that there are things which I could have done differently, perhaps to ease some of his suffering enough to give him the will to keep going, but when I have these thoughts I remind myself that the past is subjective, because it is made up of our memories alone. Our memories are often sculpted by our own emotional state, sometimes to paint ourselves in the best or worst possible light. If I were self-destructive I would expend huge amounts of energy blaming myself, flogging myself, and my life would be one vicious circle of self-recrimination, blame and negativity.

I accept responsibility in part for Alan' death in the sense that I was part of the environment that made him who he was. Our relationship wasn't perfect; at times I couldn't understand why he was so angry and this lack of understanding could lead to conflict. Over the years I have observed that some days one's mind will put entirely different spins on events, merely to suit whatever emotional state one is in at the time. On a good day I can dwell on the recollection of a shared childhood without any great sense of loss. On a bad day I may ask myself what if I had done X or Y and whether it would have made any difference. Most days I thank whoever is responsible for every moment I spend on this earth.

In the year Alan died I was lucky enough to fall truly in love for the first time. I met a wonderfully gentle and kind girl with a smile uncannily like my own, who reminded me that there are untold joys to be had on this earth. Admittedly, I was quite vulnerable at the time, but simply knowing her taught me that just as there are extremes of sorrow in life, there are also extremes of joy. I often find it curious that the two events occurred in the same year. Another shared aspect of these two important relationships – with my brother and with the girl in question – was that I eventually had to let both of them go and concentrate on getting on with my own life, and appreciate the immeasurable gift of being a living, breathing human being.

David

Seven years on and how has it changed me? Apart from the expanding black hole left behind in the years after the indescribable wrench when Alan chose to leave this life early, that immense experience of pain has altered both my personality and the way I live. I have become simultaneously more selective and less tolerant, primarily of humanity's inability to behave like 'decent human beings' towards each other, whether through their actions, words or attitudes. I am also intolerant of what some individuals – in what is a ridiculously vulgar and overly-affluent society – might perceive as problems in their lives. It has to be genuinely serious before I can, or even want to listen to it. The black wrench of Alan's death gave me perspective. Alan taught me, through his self-murder, that life is short, and I know that he didn't get enough out of his.

I have become a lot more focussed on what I want in my realm and aware of what I'm just not prepared to accept or entertain. Life is short. My experience of life has become a lot more lucid, as is the awareness of the transience of our presence on this earth. I find myself constantly pushing to clear away the artificial, to give what is natural space to breathe. I have left the city behind – the chaos, the distraction, the disturbance, the plastic, the false, the consumption, the products – in search of a more fundamental and balanced existence, and I have found a peaceful 'clearing in the woods' where I have the mental space to tune in to what is real, to enjoy the sunshine for whatever time I have in this life. The pain of losing Alan has brought me to a place where I feel alive, where I have woken up and where I truly appreciate what we have in this life of ours.

Stephen

A few months after Alan's death I began to have dreams that he came back. These were not frequent, but they were memorable. In each I dreamed that Alan was home – sometimes I saw him and sometimes I just knew he was there – and everything was just as it had been before. I felt so overjoyed, like a kid at Christmas time. I would just keep repeating, 'He's back, he's back', to everyone I met. Then at some point in my dream I would realise that Alan was dead and a gulf opened within me. I would let out a scream that came from my very core. This would begin in my dream and, I'm told, escape out of me into my bedroom. I would wake up feeling just as I did on the day I was told he was dead.

After one of these dreams I was meditating and I had a vision of Alan surrounded by angels; they were behind him, supporting him as he walked up to heaven. I know that this imagery is a bit clichéd (at least, it is for me), but what I felt was most important: that he was safe and in a good place. This knowing/feeling settled into every part of my awareness. I know in my living soul that what I felt is real.

I believe that I will never fully heal within myself as a result of Alan's death. In a way I feel my heart is cracked. I cannot show you how this really feels, but I feel it every day. Something just has not felt right since his death, as if I am not who I should be, if that makes any sense. I do, however, draw strength from this, because by not trying to be whole or right, or whatever you wish to call it, I can live with a certain peace, which only comes after the shock, anger and confusion and everything else that comes with somebody choosing to leave their life and their family behind. I could write about the things that I have done in my life since, but it's not really important to the reader. So, how to explain the most important inner journey as I hurtled from the day of his death until now? One of the most obvious things I have been faced with is that I cannot control others' choices, no matter what that choice is, and also that separation through death is inevitable. At times I go through life erecting illusions of control just to make myself feel comfortable.

Maybe I come across as being depressed or not enjoying my life – this is not true. I have lived a very full life and I have laughed heartily, but somewhere inside there is always a twinge, something slightly sour. Brazilians have a word for it, '*saudade*', like a kind of bittersweet homesickness or when you miss someone, even though you are moving on. The word does not have a direct translation into English and maybe that is what the feeling is – untranslatable.

At the funeral I remember someone saying that we will never know why Alan chose to end his life. I know that Alan was a sensitive person who hid his vulnerability under a layer of part cool and part irrepressible madness. He was such a 'character'. He developed creative and hilarious ways to keep people around him, but also to keep them locked out.

The last time I saw Alan we were watching television together in the living room. Out of nowhere he said to me, 'Steve, what am I going to do with my life?' I was quite shocked because I knew how much it took for Alan to be so straight. I treated his question like fine china and I tried to give him the best advice that I could. In hindsight, it gave me an inkling into the kind of world he was living in at the time. Maybe it was one where there was no path open before him. Maybe, no matter how hard he tried, he just couldn't imagine himself in a place where he felt safe, on top of things or feeling whole and connected.

I'm using feelings here that I have experienced myself, and I have been on the precipice a few times, not knowing why this was until it was pointed out to me by family, friends or counsellors. The reason I never jumped or fell was that, each time I had the most unbearable, lonely and painfully dark night, I locked down on one thought: after this night there is morning and the chance that things can change in a split second. I was never engulfed completely because I had hope. This was sometimes self-generated, at other times I just threw it all at God, and then sometimes it was provided by the loving people around me. I think that what Alan had lost sight of for too long was hope.

I am not ashamed to talk about my own journey through depression because I know that I'm part of a pretty big club out there! This journey for me has reached a healthy conclusion. I have learned so many important lessons from it and I am very thankful for this, but I never want to go through it again. I rarely get so down these days that I feel overwhelmed, but if I do feel down I know that it is temporary. I don't believe that life is about being happy, but about being able to cope with both happiness and sadness and every emotion in between.

I recognise the many blessings that came after Alan's death and I am thankful for them. I feel closer to my parents and siblings, we 'mind' each other when minding is needed and we always make sure to say 'I love you' – that is the most important thing as far as I am concerned.

I think about death a lot and have done since Alan left us. I don't see it looming over me or anything like that. I am aware that death separates us. The older, wiser part of me tells me that we are all connected through God and that death is not a destroyer, but a change in the cycle of nature. It is necessary and there must be a fundamentally important reason that death exists. There is also the child-like part of me who doesn't understand anything except that someone very important to my life is no longer with me. When I was in the delivery room watching our first child being born I was shocked at how natural it all felt, and I like to think that dying is like that for everyone, no matter how we choose to go – shockingly simple.

Íde

Alan was my first love and I will never forget him. It is impossible to do so because of the huge impact he has had on my life. I was eighteen when I met Alan, and only knew him for fifteen months, but in that time we became incredibly close – often too close – and during his darkest moments he would try to push me away in his attempt to protect me. But I was relentless and would not give up.

To the outside world Alan was fun-loving and was often the centre of attention, but to a select few he showed a very different side to his personality. He did tell me that at some point he would take his life and I knew he was serious. I tried to get him to seek help, but he believed that talking to me was enough. When Alan did leave I went through the normal grieving process that anyone goes through, but the guilt that I felt was immense. It took me a very long time to accept that I had done all I could to help him.

My early twenties were a blur. I don't know how I kept going sometimes as I became engulfed with sadness. I withdrew into myself and any happiness I experienced was short-lived, mainly because I relied on others to make me happy. It was difficult for people to be close to me; I was hard work. It wasn't until three years ago when I finally made the decision to open up and talk to a counsellor on a regular basis that things changed. I had been pre-scribed anti-depressants on and off for a few years, however, talking to someone so freely and without judgement was the turning point for me. I realised through the coun-selling process that the only person responsible for my own happiness was me. I figured out who I was and what I wanted to be. After that, people seemed to gravitate towards me because I was not unconsciously pushing them away. I made new friends, reconnected with old ones and instead of being on the periphery of a social cir-cle, my newfound self-confidence allowed me to take a lead role.

Losing Alan made me a more compassionate person, which is an invaluable tool in my work as a veterinary nurse and student of veterinary medicine. I am stronger than ever and can cope with any tough situations that life throws at me; I can adapt and look for the positives. Alan gave me a simple silver ring to celebrate a year together, which never leaves my finger, and now when I think of him I feel grateful and honoured to have been part of his life. There are still times when the hurt I experienced comes flooding back. Something as simple as hearing a song he used to sing can trigger it all again, but it is a sadness that is a reminder of how lucky I am; I have come a long way and I am hopeful.

A Transformative Pain

I would love to end this book by saying to those who have experienced the loss of a child that eventually the pain goes away. As I have experienced so far, one moves on from the acute agony of the loss to what I can only describe as a dull ache, an ache that does not cripple, but that allows the growth of empathy, tolerance, compassion and understanding; ultimately, a positively transformative pain.

Only a month ago we had the wonderful surprise of a visit from Stephen, who came from the Philippines with his little daughter Ella, our first grandchild, to spend a month with us. To add to our joy, Dave decided to come home from Denmark for a few days, which meant that we were all together as a family for the first time in a couple of years. Niall held a party for us in his garden and looking around at my family in these beautiful surroundings, the sunny day completed the picture – but the sunny day did not complete the picture ... to have Alan there would have completed the picture.